RealityCharting

Seven Steps to Effective Problem-Solving and Strategies for Personal Success

By Dean L. Gano

D1089603

First Edition

Apollonian Publications, LLC
Richland, Washington
USA

To all who value learning

Table of Contents

Preface

At the time of my first book, *Apollo Root Cause Analysis*, published in 1999, the Internet was just beginning to take off and most computers where big bulky things. There was talk of a paperless society and newspapers and books were doomed. Well, it has taken more years than the pundits predicted, but today newspapers are going out of business and electronic book sales increased 400% in 2010.

As you will see in this book, which is being published traditionally and electronically, technology has not only advanced the way we consume information, it has allowed us to communicate much more effectively. Specifically, technology allowed us to create RealityCharting® software back in 2001 and a new online learning module in 2011, both of which allow a more effective use of our valuable time.

The RealityCharting® software allows us, for the first time in history, to easily communicate the causal relationships of any event. Unfortunately, learning how to use the software and the process has historically been difficult and time consuming. The RealityCharting process was first taught in a classroom setting of lecture and exercises and took two days to complete. In 2009, we became aware of a new way to teach, using electronic media, that is better than classroom style learning because it is challenging, interactive, allows learning by failing, provides instant feedback, and facilitates working at your own pace. It has the ability to redo or quickly review and there is no advancement until the prerequisites are learned. There is a focus on learning everything in each lesson and by working exercises that prove you learned the lesson; there is no need for a test—you either learn and show competence in all of the subject matter or you don't move forward. Because of this new learning module, most people can learn the process and the software in half the time (or less) than what it has traditionally taken in a classroom setting. It also ensures uniformity of a quality experience as opposed to the possibility of an inexperienced teacher butchering the intent of the lesson.

Since we know that some people want to know more about the subject than just the basic process and how to use a software application,

I have written this book to meet that need. While it contains some of the basic information that was in my previous book, it has a lot of new material and includes links to the interactive online learning modules provided in the new software as a way to usher in this new learning style. So, this is much more than your usual book—it is an interactive adventure into the world of effective problem solving that will change the way you think, communicate, and make decisions.

Acknowledgments

This book is the product of many years of study driven by my unwillingness to accept contradictions. I see contradictions where most people do not, so I have studied the sciences, religion, and philosophy, and I am grateful for all those who have gone before me in trying to figure out the notion of causation. Aristotle, Aquinas, Pascal, Newton, Buddha, and several modern players like Peter M. Senge, Charles H. Kepner, and Benjamin B. Tregoe have provided valuable steppingstones to the message of this book. I am indebted to my students around the world who have asked invaluable questions and challenged me to know more. Without their questioning attitude, I would never have come this far.

I am particularly grateful for the intellectual stimulation of a few close colleagues, namely Larry Reising, Tim Adams, and my son, Wesley J. Gano. Along with many others who I have encountered along the way, my son Wesley has provided an honest intellectual sounding board often necessary to break outside the envelope of conventional wisdom. Tim Adams is an engineer at NASA who has mentored me for the last fifteen years on everything from Probability Risk Analysis to effective learning strategies. His advice and guidance has been invaluable on more than one occasion. Larry Reising of World-Interplay is a RealityCharting Master Instructor and was instrumental in helping me bring the new learning modules found in this book to fruition. He is dedicated to continuous learning and fundamentally understands the need to innovate.

I had many new challenges along my path, so I am grateful to my wife, Mary, for understanding my needs and to my parents for teaching me to greet every new challenge with a positive attitude.

Honest comments are hard to come by when one presumes to write a book, so I am very thankful for the editorial reviews and critical comments provided by those listed above as well as Jim Davis, Mark Hall, Ned Callahan and Mick Drew.

Editors always win in the end and for this we writers are thankful. I want to acknowledge my editors, Paul McIntire and Sue Gano. I want to thank them for their patience, dedication to a smooth-flowing book, and for putting up with my protestations and analytical mindset.

I also want to thank Ethan Edwards of Allen Interactions for teaching me how to create effective interactive online training.

Introduction

Asking why things happen is an essential part of being human. When we ask why something happened, we are looking for causes to help us understand reality. But what is reality? How can we know it? What is its structure and is there a single reality that we can all see? As you will learn in this book and the accompanying electronic exercises, there is no single reality, but you will learn how to create a common reality by defining evidenced-based causal relationships. With this common reality, we can predict the outcome of certain scenarios, which allows us to recognize various patterns and thus control the causes to guide us in reaching our goals. The better we understand causal relationships, the higher the probability of attaining our goals both as a group and individually.

The purpose of this book is to help you better understand the notion of reality and provide the basis for teaching everyone how to think causally using a simple process and some very helpful software.

One of the fundamental reasons we are challenged in understanding reality is that it is very complex and our minds simply cannot deal with the complexity without some help. To make matters worse, our language and communication skills have heretofore prevented us from expressing the complexity that is reality—more on this later. However, with the advent of the computer and the creation of a simple tool called RealityCharting® we are now able to unlock the complexity of reality and more importantly provide all stakeholders of a given problem the ability to express and combine their realities. By creating a common reality that defines the known causal relationships of a given event, stakeholders can easily come to agreement on which causes can be controlled and how to control them, to meet their common objectives.

At the heart of this book is a new way of communicating that is revolutionizing the way people solve problems and make decisions together. Imagine your next decision-making meeting where everyone is in agreement with the causes of the problem and the effectiveness of the proposed corrective actions—no conflicts, arguments, or power politics! This is the promise of the RealityCharting process.

RealityCharting

As thinking animals, we understand our world by giving objects names (called "nouns") and we describe actions using various words that we call "verbs." We express variations of these nouns and verbs by adding qualifiers, which we call "adjectives" and "adverbs." We then assemble these words into sentences and tell stories (made of many such sentences) to communicate with others what we think we know. All humans interact with their environment in a slightly different way and thus develop a unique perspective or reality. By sharing our unique reality with others we gradually increase our collective understanding of the world we live in. However, not all of us are good at sharing what we think we know, nor are we always correct in our understanding. As a result, we often find our realities in conflict with others, which can result in ineffective problem solving and can sometimes have serious consequences. Humans have always debated the notion of right and wrong and this conflict is at the core of ineffective problem solving. The cause of these conflicts is a clash of realities, so before we can expect to find effective solutions to human problems, we need to find a way to create a common reality that everyone can agree on.

The basis for a common reality is what we call a "principle," which by definition is a causal relationship that works the same way every time regardless of the observer—the law of gravity is such a principle. As you will learn in this book, several wise men, who have come before us, have defined some fundamental laws or principles of causation that we can use to better understand reality. At the peril of all humankind, we have not learned these fundamentals well and we continue to ignore these great insights—this error will be corrected by reading this book.

The RealityCharting process described herein is based on these fundamental principles from the ancients and thus provides a principle-based approach to understanding and solving human problems. By expressing the causal relationships of a given event that includes all stakeholders' reality, we can capitalize on the knowledge of the many to create a more complete reality. Not "Reality" with a capital R, because there is no such thing, but a common reality that everyone can see and agree with.

Personal Success

Success in life is driven by the human need to be happy, regardless of how you define success or happiness. Among other things, happiness/success is caused by the absence of stress. To avoid stress we attempt to create stress-free conditions by controlling the causes of stress in our lives. To be effective at removing stressful conditions we need to understand the causal relationships that initiate stress in the first place. While we seem to know that removing stress makes us happier, research shows that stress actually damages the mechanisms that control the division of living cells in our bodies. This damage results in a shorter life due to cancer and early aging. On the flip side, research also shows that those who have more control over their lives have less stress and live longer. So, personal success and individual happiness are directly related to understanding the causal relationships that govern stress.

As you will see, the RealityCharting process is very simple and can be used on any event-type problem. But this book is more than just a way of learning how to be a better problem solver. It will take you on a journey of principles and philosophy that can lead to a better understanding of the big questions in life, like what is reality and why are we here?

1

Paradigm Shift

It becomes obvious that if we want to make relatively minor changes in our lives, we can perhaps appropriately focus on our attitudes and behaviors. But if we want to make significant quantum change, we need to work on our basic paradigms.

—Stephen R. Covey

In every human endeavor, a critical component to our success is our ability to solve problems. Unfortunately, we often set ourselves up to fail with our various problem-solving strategies and our inherent prejudices. We typically rely on what we believe to be common sense, storytelling, and categorizing to resolve our problems. Conventional wisdom has us believe that problem solving is inherent to the subject at hand—the doctor solves medical problems, the mechanic fixes our car, etc. Using the strategies most of us have learned in our lives typically leads to conformity, which brings complacency and mediocrity. This chapter will expose the ineffective strategies that prevent us from being effective problem solvers.

In his highly successful book, *The Seven Habits of Highly Effective People*, Stephen Covey so eloquently shares the notion of a paradigm shift. This is the big "aha" moment where we realize that what we have been doing all these years was fundamentally wrong and more importantly that a new understanding can totally change our effectiveness.

Thomas Kuhn first introduced the term "paradigm shift" in his book, *The Structure of Scientific Revolutions*. Mr. Kuhn explains that at the core of all science is the need to prove the current theory wrong and that breaking with old beliefs and accepting totally new and different views of the subject at hand causes nearly every scientific breakthrough. Indeed, as you will learn from one of the principles of causation, the more we know, the more we know we don't know. Or to put it another way, the more we know, the dumber we get. It is not the pursuit of existing knowledge that makes us effective problem solvers, but the pursuit of understanding our ignorance—to find answers to what we don't know. And since the human condition is wrought with complacency, ignorance, and arrogance, this can be a hard pill to swallow.

I first discovered this problem with conventional problem-solving methods in 1979 while working in the nuclear power industry and investigating the incident at the Three Mile Island Nuclear Power Plant. As you may recall, they experienced a reactor core meltdown and released a small amount of radioactive gasses to the local environment. I was involved in an industry group trying to understand what went wrong and to use the lessons learned from the event to make nuclear power even safer than it was at the time. In the process of evaluating and performing root cause analysis on the various failures that occurred at the Three Mile Island Plant, I discovered that the problem-solving methods of the time were grossly inadequate—and so began a thirty-plus-year journey of studying human problem solving.

By first recognizing the failed strategies of the past, I began an evolution of thought to a new paradigm about problem solving—a paradigm shift that has the potential to fundamentally change the way humans forever evaluate and solve human problems of all kinds. Being an analytic by nature and an engineer by training, I was surprised to find that there were no common or universally accepted fundamental principles of causation. Most of the problem-solving processes, and certainly the most popular ones, were people centric and subjective rather than principle based and objective. In shock, I began doing research on human problem solving and read many books, but did not find any evidence of fundamental principles of causation, so I came up with my own. I experimented and refined them while teaching a form of root cause analysis to various companies throughout the world until I found universal acceptance. But it wasn't until several years later, with the growth of the Internet and the Google search engine, that I was able to do an extensive search of the subject. To my delight, I discovered that a few individuals had made huge paradigm shifts regarding causation in the last 2,600 years. While I was confident in the principles I had defined, I was uncomfortable with seemingly being alone in my protestations against conventional wisdom. As discussed in the next sections, I discovered I was not alone, but rather in the presence of good company.

Traditional Problem-Solving Strategies

The most basic approach to problem solving, discussed throughout history, from Buddha[1] to present time, is *causal observation*. Sometimes referred to as "street smarts," this strategy calls for observing our environment with an eye toward cause-and-effect relationships. For example, if you see smoke, you know there may be a fire, because you understand the set of causes associated with smoke. While causal observation serves us well, there are no commonly accepted principles of causation to actually guide us in this strategy. Instead we use various other strategies, such as linear thinking, categorization, storytelling, common sense, and various forms of so-called "root cause analysis," that focus on finding root causes rather than effective solutions. Let's examine each of these failed strategies.

Linear Thinking

Like a string of falling dominos, when we simply ask why, why, why, like the conventional Five Whys method, we believe that A caused B, B caused C, C caused D[2], and somewhere at the end of this causal chain there is a magical single cause that started everything, i.e., the root cause.[3]

In the thirteenth century, St. Thomas Aquinas of Sicily taught us the fallacy of this strategy when he proposed that "potency cannot reduce itself to act."[4] Or, as he clarified with this example, "the copper cannot become a statue by its own existence." It requires the conditional cause of the copper's existence *and* the actions of a sculptor. Unfortunately, this simple and important observation has not been understood or incorporated into everyday thinking, and most people continue to see the world linearly.

Categorization

Categorizing causes is a very common event-type problem-solving strategy. Instead of identifying the actions and conditions of each effect, as St. Thomas Aquinas would have us do, this strategy places causes in a predefined box, which implies some causal information.

Categorical schemes like fishbone diagrams, management oversight and risk tree (MORT)[5], and cause trees of every ilk[5] prescribe a hierarchical set of causal factors based on the reality of one person or a group of individuals[6], depending on the source. Using a tree of causal factors (not causes) usually starting with the categories of manpower, machinery, materials, methods, and environment, these methods provide a list with subcategories and sub-subcategories, branching like the roots of a tree so the sophomoric analogy goes. These lists, which range from one page to several, often claim to include all the possible causal factors governing human activities. The stated goal of these methods is to find the root cause or causes. This is accomplished by asking if the problem at hand encompasses any of the causal factors on the predefined list. Each category is examined and evaluated to determine if the causal factor was involved in the event. If any correlations are found, the stakeholders discuss them and vote on which causal factors are the "root causes" and then solutions are applied to these so-called "root causes." It is important to note at this point that these are not causes they are evaluating; these are causal factors and there is no attempt to identify causal relationships—only to determine if this category was a factor in the event being scrutinized. Some of these methods are bold enough to provide predefined solutions for *your* problem—as if they understand the details of *your* business and the people involved. While these methodologies provide some structure to the problem-solving process and provide a reference list of possible causal factors that may help you discover some things you did not know, categorical methods are not principle-based and thus create many other problems as discussed below.

In addition to what we learned from St. Thomas Aquinas that every effect has at least two causes, as early as the fifth century BC, Buddhist writings reveal that "as a net is made up of a series of knots, so everything in the world is connected by a series of knots."[7] At the heart of this observation is a fundamental principle that all causes are part of a very complex, infinite set of causes, yet we ignore this simple observation when using prescribed categorical problem-solving strategies.

Buddha went on to state that duality and categorization are simple-minded constructs that ignore the reality of causal relationships.[8] For example, is it good or bad that the lion eats the gazelle? Neither—it is an event consisting of many complex and interactive causal relationships. Using the duality of good or bad/right or wrong simply puts the problem in a category and ignores the causal relationships of the event.

The categorization strategy is part of a larger, very simplistic strategy, which goes on to suggest that if we can categorize something, we can implement standard solutions. For example, if something is bad, we must act against it, or if something is good, we should revel in it. Or, if the training is inadequate, we can make it better, but "inadequate" is not an actionable cause. Categorical strategies may have worked fine in a simpler past, but in today's world, understanding the causal relationships of significant events can make the difference between extinction and survival, not just in business, but personally and as a species as well.

However, like the causal observation strategy, categorizing is at the core of pattern recognition, which is a fundamental biological process built into the genome of higher life forms, so it is only natural that we would develop methods like causal factors charts. Because categorization is a natural brain process, people who use these methods think they are effective. When asked to explain *all* the causal relationships of a given event, they can't do it, but they usually have a good understanding of the main causes and may even be able to explain some of the causal relationships. At the same time, they are unable to effectively communicate them, because these relationships reside in the mind, not in a graphical form that can be shared and openly discussed with other stakeholders. Categorical processes simply do not delineate causal relationships.[8] When other stakeholders cannot clearly see the reasons (causal relationships) behind a decision to change, or are not able to share their causal understanding of the problem, they are often very reluctant to accept the proposed solutions—often resulting in conflict and disagreement.

A classic example of this "causal factor" strategy can be seen in the *Deepwater Horizon Accident Investigation Report* presented by British Petroleum in September 2010. In this report, they explain that there were four "critical factors" involved when the Deepwater Horizon Oil Drilling Rig caught fire and subsequently caused the largest oil spill in the history of the United States. The critical factors identified were:

1. Well integrity was not established or failed.
2. Hydrocarbons entered the well undetected and well control was lost.

3. Hydrocarbons ignited on Deepwater Horizon.
4. Blowout preventer did not seal the well.

They also identified "eight key findings."

1. The annulus cement barrier did not isolate the hydrocarbons.
2. The shoe track barriers did not isolate the hydrocarbons.
3. The negative-pressure test was accepted although well integrity had not been established.
4. Influx was not recognized until hydrocarbons were in the riser.
5. Well control response actions failed to regain control of the well.
6. Diversion to the mud gas separator resulted in gas venting onto the oil rig.
7. The fire and gas detection and suppression systems did not prevent hydrocarbon ignition.
8. The blowout preventer (BOP) emergency mode did not seal the well.

While the report goes on to provide many causes for each of these categorical factors or findings, the investigation uses conventional problem-solving strategies to examine the causes. As a result, the analysis is incomplete and very difficult to understand. By focusing on these four "critical factors" and "eight key findings," the investigation team missed the opportunity to clearly understand all the causal relationships and more importantly to effectively communicate the many causal relationships they did understand.

To read the entire Deepwater Horizon Accident report, go to http://Coach.RealityCharting.com/book/Deepwater-Horizon.

Storytelling

Throughout history, our primary form of communication has been through storytelling. This strategy describes an event by relating people (who elements), places (where elements), and things (what elements) in a linear time frame (when elements). Stories start in the past and move linearly toward the present, while cause-and-effect relationships always start with the undesirable effect (the present) and go back in time, branching with at least two causes each time we ask why—two totally opposite concepts.

In addition to using causal factors analysis, the *Deepwater Horizon Accident Investigation Report* presented by British Petroleum uses storytelling, barrier analysis, and a crude form of fault tree analysis to understand the event. The following is an example of how they used storytelling to analyze one of the reasons why the blowout preventer did not seal the well and oil was released.

> "Solenoid Valve 103 Condition: During the yellow pod test performed by Transocean and Cameron after the accident, both coils on solenoid valve 103 failed to energize, suggesting electrical faults. The investigation team found no evidence that this failure occurred after the accident; rather, the team concluded that this failure condition very likely existed prior to the accident. (*Refer to 5.1 Maintenance* of this analysis) A faulty solenoid valve 103 would mean that the yellow pod could not have performed the Automatic Mode Function (to isolate the well), as no pilot signal could have been sent to the pilot-operated control valve to activate the high-pressure Blind Shear Ram close function. As described in *5.5 Monitoring and Diagnostic Capability* of this analysis, the rig's Blowout Preventer control diagnostic system should have been capable of remotely detecting the faulty solenoid valve and recording it on the system event logger."

Furthermore, *Section 5.1 Maintenance* of this analysis provides the following story:

> "In September 2009, A BP rig audit team conducted an audit of Deepwater Horizon. This audit included the maintenance management system for the Blowout Preventer. One finding was, "Overdue maintenance in excess of 30 days was considered excessive, totaling 390 jobs and 3,545 man hours. Many of the overdue routines were high priority." This audit, which the team performed at the end of the rig out-of-service period for ten-year maintenance and inspection, identified thirty-one findings that were related to the well control system maintenance. Of these, six findings related to Blowout Preventer maintenance; all findings were outstanding as of December 2009.

The following maintenance-related audit findings were associated with the Blowout Preventer.

- *The subsea maintenance personnel recorded well control-related equipment maintenance manually on separate spreadsheets and in the daily logbook, instead of the Transocean maintenance management system (RMS-II). This practice made it difficult to track Blowout Preventer maintenance.*
- *The lower (test), middle and upper ram bonnets had not been recertified since 2000. The original equipment manufacturer (OEM) and API-recommended recertification period is five years.*
- *The maintenance records did not substantiate that Transocean was in conformance with its five-year replacement policy for replacement of high-pressure hoses."*

The report goes on to list many other maintenance deficiencies in this same storytelling fashion.

To wit, *Section 5.5 Monitoring and Diagnostic Capability* not only provides more storytelling, but most disturbingly fails to identify critical causes as you will see from the following:

"Diagnostics of the Blowout Preventer control system were available to the rig crew and subsea personnel through an alarm indication system and event logger. The alarm system was integrated into the driller's control panel and into the Tool Pusher Control Panel (TCP). The event logger was located in the subsea workshop, and it may never be recovered.

The control panels displayed alarms in two ways: through the alarm display and through an array of dedicated alarm lights. The alarm display provided alarm tables that were programmed into the programmable logic controller (PLC), based on the importance of the component being monitored. It displayed alarm notifications for low accumulator pressure, PLC system failure, pod SEM mismatch, coil fault in the active pod, hydraulic pressure unit not available, low pilot pressure and a number of other parameters. The dedicated alarm lights displayed the most critical fault alarms selected and pre-programmed from the PLC alarm tables.

The control system was capable of identifying the coil defects in solenoid valves 103 and 3A in the yellow pod and logging them in the event logger. A failure mode effects and criticality analysis (FMECA) performed as part of the Blowout Preventer assurance analysis of *Deepwater Horizon* Blowout Preventer stack identified this failure mode. As stated in the FMECA report, when this failure is detected, the mitigation is "Switch to alternate pod, secure well and pull the Lower Marine Riser Package."

Even though this investigation is not a causal analysis, the story leaves us hanging on the next why question. Why didn't someone see or do anything about the failed solenoid valve, which they state would have been identified by an alarm at two different control panels and the event logger? There is no discussion as to whether they even made an attempt to ask the operators if such an alarm had been identified or if the operators ever looked at the event logger. Instead we are left with a dead-end cause path.

More importantly, by using storytelling to analyze the event, the causes that are identified in the report are very difficult to follow and hence hinder our ability to understand the relationships between all the causes and hence provide an honest critique of the analysis. The investigators may very well understand all the causal relationships, but because they are not presented causally we will never know and peer reviews will certainly result in many questions. Furthermore, when you discover a huge gap in the story such as why the solenoid valve failure went undetected, the entire analysis becomes suspect.

To better understand the difference between storytelling and causal analysis, compare what you just read about the oil release and the following causal analysis shown below, that was derived from the investigation report. The page numbers provided in the evidence balloons under each cause are the page numbers from the Deepwater Horizon Accident report.

Hopefully you can see from this comparison that a Realitychart provides a much clearer understanding of the event than storytelling provides.

In our normal conversations, stories are usually void of causes and also tend to leave out causal evidence. They often use categories, innuendo, and symbolism to infer causal relationships. Stories by their very nature are often focused on human actions while ignoring the necessary conditional causes. For example, a story might tell of a fire being started by an arsonist, but will not mention that the cause of the fire also included

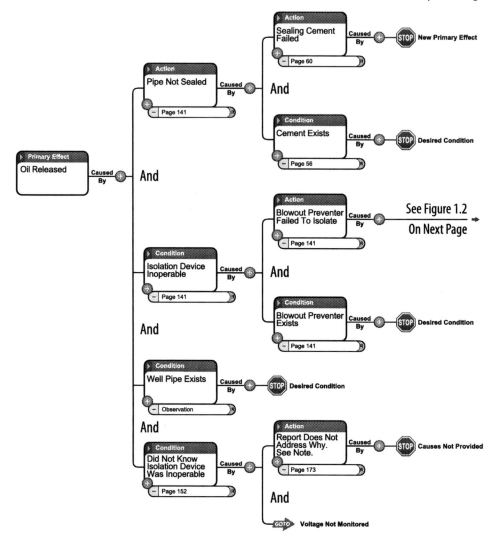

Figure 1.1. Realitychart Page 1: Deepwater Horizon Oil Spill

the conditional causes of flammable material, a match, and oxygen and that all these things occurred at the same point in time and space.

While conditional causes may not be important in an entertaining story, they are often the source of the most effective solutions to a problem because they are more easily controlled than human actions. For example, to prevent fires we often separate the conditional causes in time and space by not allowing the fire source (match or flame) and the combustible material to be in the same proximity at the same time.

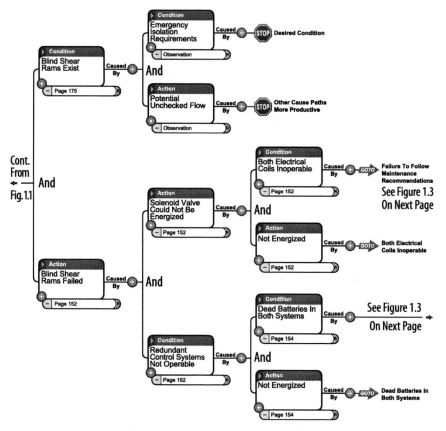

Figure 1.2. Realitychart Page 2: Deepwater Horizon Oil Spill

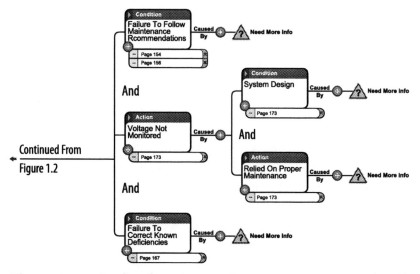

Figure 1.3. Realitychart Page 3: Deepwater Horizon Oil Spill

Common Sense

When the jury in the Oklahoma City bombing trial could not decide on the death penalty for convicted terrorist Terry Nichols, a jurist lamented, "If I learned anything from this, it is that two people can look at the same situation and see two completely different things." Indeed, how could this happen? Where is the common sense? The evidence was obvious, the decision clear. What's wrong with some people anyway? We usually end this line of thinking by concluding that some people just don't have any common sense.

When asked, most of us believe we have our world pretty well figured out and are good problem solvers. We also believe that most of those around us are equally good at problem solving. In fact, we seem to believe that reality is the same for everyone. We believe that if we are able to think of it, it must be common to everyone else. Sometimes, when people don't act according to our preconceived ideas, we say they don't have any common sense. We may even question our friendship with them because we certainly don't want to associate with idiots.

Common sense is defined as the common feeling of humanity. With tongue in cheek, it can be defined as that body of knowledge that my friends and I share. In either definition, it is anything but common because we don't have the same friends or the same feelings as the next person. Common sense is often used as an excuse for explaining why others do not "see" things the way we do and then punishing them for it. I once heard a chemical plant manager say, "Since when did our people start checking their common sense at the gate?"

Each one of us is unique, and our genetic building blocks and the environment in which our perceptions were developed cause that uniqueness. Exploring why our perceptions are unique helps us debunk the notion of common sense.

Perception exists within each mind and is a four-step process:

1. Receiving data from the senses.
2. Processing the data in the mind to form knowledge.
3. Developing operational strategies as they relate to what we already know.
4. Establishing conclusions and prototypical truths.

Our Unique Senses

Receiving data from the senses is unique to each one of us. Our sight, hearing, touch, smell, and taste are different than other people—

sometimes significantly different. Some people need glasses to see, others don't. Our senses are developed early in life and are a direct function of our environment. Research indicates that children who are visually entertained in the first year of life establish more neural connections and hence have more active minds.[9]

The brain reserves certain areas for each sense. The visual cortex, for example, is located at the rear of the brain, the sensory cortex along the sides, and so forth. As each sense is stimulated, neurological connections are being made in the respective portion of the brain. Patterns are recognized and value assigned to each stimulus in each sensory portion of the brain.

The development of each sensory portion of the brain is a function of the genetic structure of the mind and environmental stimulation. Each sense is on a genetically coded timeline for development. Once that time frame has passed, the sense will all but stop developing.

The acuity of each sense depends on the richness of the environment to which it is exposed during the window of opportunity. For example, if a child is completely blindfolded for the first three to six years of life, the sight portion of the brain will not develop and the child will never see, even though the eyes are completely functional. Physicians have found that covering one eye of an infant for a short period of time (a week or more) will likely cause that eye to be less developed than the other one, resulting in the need for glasses[9] and in a different perspective of the world.

And so, on goes the development of our senses, such that every person senses the world differently and creates his or her own unique sensory perception.

Processing Data

In the thought-provoking book, *Descartes' Error*,[10] Antonio R. Damasio, M.D., provides great insights into the workings of the mind. Dr. Damasio and others have found the causes of learning in the physical nature of the mind. The brain is made up of billions of cells known as "neurons," which consist of a cell body, a main output fiber called an "axon," and input fibers known as "dendrites." These neurons are interconnected in circuits and systems within the brain. Brain functions, including our ideas and thoughts, occur when neurons become active through an electrochemical process. Each time we have a new thought or experience something new, axons and dendrites "connect" via a synapse as part of this electrochemical process. If the same thought or experience is repeated, the same physical connections become stronger. Figure 1.4 shows a simplified version of this process.

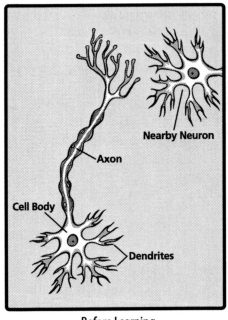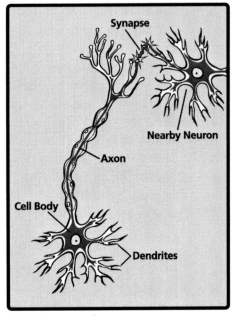

Before Learning	After Learning

Figure 1.4.   Impact of Repeated Stimulation on Learning

This is not to suggest that one connection constitutes a specific piece of conscious knowledge. It is much more complicated than that, but the observation that these neurological connections occur during learning and actually grow in size and strength with repeated exposure to a given stimulus means that we have a predilection or bias when given the same stimulus. Hence our perceptions are hard-wired.

Scientists have recently discovered there are other biological processes that also strengthen these connections. Without going into all the detailed causes, we now know that new ideas require new connections and therefore new ideas are at a disadvantage to old ideas. This does not mean we cannot learn new things, but it does mean we must remove or modify existing connections in order to register new thoughts. Old connections that are no longer needed are actually dissolved (physically) by special compounds in the brain.[11] These normal brain processes help explain the notion of truth or opinion and we can now understand that for the mind to accept a new truth, we not only have to create new neural connections, we have to abandon the existing ones and that takes time and energy, which an economizing brain is reluctant to provide.

Also, as data or information is sensed, it is processed into categories for economy of thought. We assign nouns to things and verbs to actions.

Everything is sorted, prioritized, and possibly stored. Categorization in the mind is physical. Nouns are stored in one physical location of the brain and verbs are stored in another location.

We all have our own interests and abilities based partly on our environment and partly on our genetic makeup. Growing up in Africa with Jane Goodall as your mother would provide you with different knowledge than if you grew up in a poor neighborhood in a large city, such as New York. The resulting personalities and perspectives would also be quite different. While we share many common characteristics, we each possess our own unique knowledge base.

Our Unique Strategies

A key aspect of perception is how we order knowledge. The ordering process is what we call "strategies." For example, an infant may learn that crying causes hunger to go away because it causes someone to feed him. From this causal relationship, children may learn the strategy of whining to get their way. Depending on reinforcement from our environment, we will adopt or abandon a given strategy.

If we obtain our goals with a given strategy, we will retain it as part of our belief system. Each strategy becomes part of the mind's operating system, and every person uses different strategies for dealing with life's problems. One person may find success in stealing, while another finds failure. Or, in the business world one person may use the strategy of building networks to advance whereas another might use the strategy of working long hours on many projects. Hence, each person will determine the "best" strategy based on his or her own experiences, where "best" is unique to each person and is centered around what works to meet their goals and objectives.

Our Unique Conclusions

The mind is continually sensing, ordering, and developing strategies. It is always open to new possibilities but to varying degrees depending on how hard-wired the existing idea is. As adults, we seek validation of existing beliefs (knowledge and strategies) and do not like change. Inherent in our operating system, however, is the prototype strategy. We know from past experience that sometimes things don't happen exactly as they did the time before so we reserve the right to change our belief system. In effect, we naturally establish prototypical truths that are the best we know now but are subject to change given strong enough reasons to do so. For example, for most of us the earth does not move under our feet and this is the truth. Anyone who has experienced an earthquake, however, knows this is not valid—the earth does move and it can move violently. If you have felt the earth move under your feet or have seen a wave in the earth move across a field, your first perception may be one of disbelief, but you soon change your belief system to accommodate the evidence.

We hold our belief systems open to change by the use of a prototypical conclusion.

Our unique perception of the world, coupled with our unique interaction strategies, combines to form unique people with unique prototypical truths. All these factors are continuously evolving, some more so than others; but there is clearly no way to be anything but unique individuals. No two people will hold the exact same set of prototypical truths, not even conjoined twins who obviously live in the same environment.

Understanding this uniqueness calls into question the notion of common sense. What does it mean to have common sense when not a single person has the same view of the world or holds the same belief system? Indeed, what is real? What is reality? Can we know it? When we use the word "reality," we assume that there is a single reality and everyone can see it. By understanding the biological impossibility of perceiving the world the same, the notion of a single reality can now be seen as the illusion it is. But don't worry—a solution is at hand.

Another element of common sense is the degree to which we hold to our beliefs. We call this "bias" or "prejudice." It seems that no matter how hard we try, sometimes it is nearly impossible to pull ourselves out of a groove or rut. This groove can be an idea, a belief, or a habit. Sometimes we remain intransigent even when the path leads directly to a harmful outcome. The kamikaze pilots in World War II or the suicide bombers of radical Islam provide a vivid example of a highly biased state.

In your daily life, consider the people who judge everything they see and proclaim it right or *wrong!* Prejudice is a natural state of being too focused on being right while ignoring a broader perspective. It is present in all humans and varies from inconvenience to the paralyzed mind of a fanatic. And understanding its causes can help us understand that it is part of being human. Understanding the physiology behind the process can help us see how easy it is to be brainwashed or to develop an intellect for music, athletics, or whatever we choose. Just like practice makes perfect in sports, repetition of an idea or thought can create a perfect reality that only exists in the mind of the one who created it. It can become real, regardless of contradictory evidence.

If we spend our lives focused on validating specific relationships, these relationships will indeed become valid. They become valid because of repeated exposure of the mind to the same conditions—we are what we feed our minds. Pick any controversial topic—extraterrestrials, evolution, creationism, or who has the best football team—and you will find proponents that know the "truth" of their position. What they don't understand is that their truth is the result of their own brainwashing. With this belief in our own truth comes the strongest of all human characteristics—denial. Denial is our strongest attribute and now that we understand how the mind works, we can see the causes of denial are also part of our biology.

So, if perception is reality and everyone's reality is unique, what is reality or truth? This question of the ages continues to haunt us, but the answer is quite simple if you can grasp the notion of relativity. Everything is relative to our own unique perceptions. We each hold our own truths, and to move to a common reality we need a process that will accommodate everyone's reality. Defining and using fundamental cause-and-effect principles, along with stated evidence for every cause, will lead to this common understanding because it will allow everyone's reality to be included in the event analysis.

Root Cause Myth

This is a common strategy found in most categorical schemes. Again, because of linear thinking, the belief is that there is a root cause at the end of a cause chain, and our goal is to find it so we can remove or control it and thus prevent the problem from recurring (which by the way is the core definition of a root cause).

Historically, we see that this strategy has been around for a long time. In the thirteenth century, St. Thomas Aquinas also stated that nothing is caused by itself, every effect has a prior cause, and therefore there has to be a first (root) cause.[12] However, as St. Thomas has already taught us, causal reality is not linear because it requires at least two causes in the form of an action and a condition for each effect. While St. Thomas Aquinas seemed to miss the contradiction of these two arguments, we can see that the fallacy of finding the rootiest of root causes is nothing new.

Reality is more like Buddha's causal net, which is similar to Figure 1.5, where we see that the minimum causal structure of every event is an

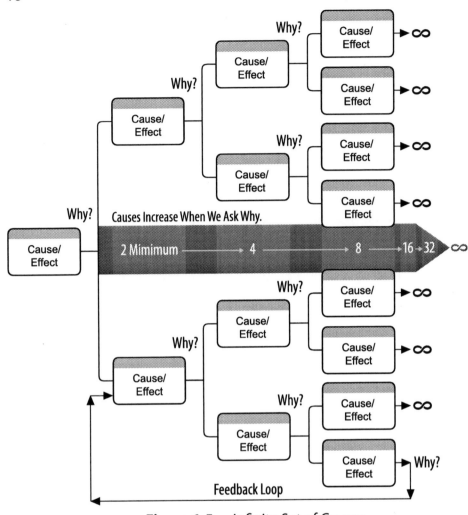

Figure 1.5.   Infinite Set of Causes

ever-increasing set of causes from two to four, to eight to sixteen, to infinity with some feedback loops included. Because there is potentially an infinite set of causes for a given event, a singular first (root) cause is not possible. Therefore, in order to ensure effective solutions we must first have a clear understanding of the known causal relationships. Then and only then can we determine which causes that if removed or controlled will prevent problem recurrence. The causes to which the solutions are associated are then, by definition, the root causes. Therefore, root causes are secondary to and contingent upon the solutions, not the object of our search, as those who use the categorical processes would have us believe.

Principles of Causation

With this abbreviated review of human problem-solving, we can see that while the great thinkers had some good ideas, the lessons of the past have not been fully incorporated into traditional problem-solving processes. The following discussion incorporates what we have learned from this stroll through history to help us define some principles of cause and effect (Figure 1.6) and use them to refine the conventional elements of effective problem solving.

We learned the first principle from Buddha and St. Thomas Aquinas, who recognized that causes are observed as a sequence in time from effect to cause. And since we can only ask why of an effect, what was previously a cause must be referred to as an effect so we can continue to ask why. Therefore, causes and effects are the same thing, only seen from a different point in time. Or, stated another way, the thing we are focusing on can be either a cause or an effect. Second, we learned from Buddha's causal net that causes and effects are part of an infinite continuum of causes—there are no laws or principles that require us to stop asking why,

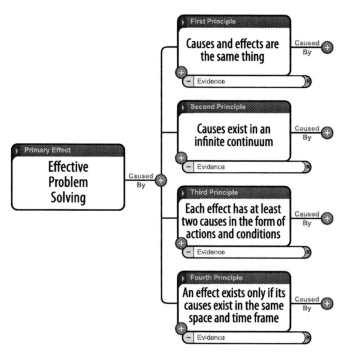

Figure 1.6. Cause-and-Effect Principles

only our own arrogance to think otherwise. The third principle, from St. Thomas Aquinas, states that each effect has at least two causes in the form of actions and conditions. While he did not require them to occur at the same point in time and space as the fourth principle states, he provided the most enlightening principle of them all—yet it has been completely overlooked by most people. The fourth principle, which states that an effect only exists if its causes exist in the same space and time frame, is self-evident in Newtonian physics.

Seven Steps to Effective Problem Solving

As discussed in the beginning of this chapter, principles are important because they hold true for every observer. To continue using people-centric problem-solving processes instead of principle-based strategies is unacceptable in the complicated world we find ourselves. Instead, we can use the cause-and-effect principles and the discussion provided herein to redefine the protocol for finding effective solutions to event-type problems.

As a minimum, effective event-type problem solving should include the following seven steps:

1. Define the problem.
2. Determine the known causal relationships to include the actions and conditions of each effect.
3. Provide a graphical representation of the causal relationships to include specific action and conditional causes.
4. Provide evidence to support the existence of each cause.
5. Determine if each set of causes is sufficient and necessary to cause the effect.
6. Provide effective solutions that remove, change, or control one or more causes of the event. Solutions must be shown to prevent recurrence, meet our goals and objectives, be within our control, and not cause other problems.
7. Implement and track the effectiveness of each solution.

Each of these steps is discussed is separate chapters of this book.

Continuous Improvement—The Essence of Quality

In our quest for continuous improvement, we must recognize failed strategies, have the courage to abandon them, embrace better ones, and forever challenge what we think we know. Who knows, if enough people discover these principles and find the courage to abandon the comforts of their own reality by accepting a new paradigm, maybe we can actually live up to the ideal that a dedication to quality requires continuous improvement.

To view a short seventeen-minute video presentation of this chapter, go to http://Coach.RealityCharting.com/book/Effective-Problem-Solving.

References

1. Luang Prinyayogavipulya. *Concise Principles of Buddhism*, second edition (1957).
2. Vincent Ryan Ruggiero *Beyond Feelings. A Guide to Critical Thinking*, seventh edition. McGraw–Hill (2004), p. 112.
3. *Stanford Encyclopedia of Philosophy*, "Causal Processes." Dec. 8, 1996 and updated Sept. 10, 2007.
4. Vernon J. Bourke. *The Pocket Aquinas*. Washington Square Press (1960), p. 67.
5. Paul F. Wilson, Larry D. Dell, and Gaylord F. Anderson. *Root Cause Analysis—A Tool for Total Quality Management*. Quality Press (1993), p. 187.
6. Paul F. Wilson, Larry D. Dell, and Gaylord F. Anderson. *Root Cause Analysis—A Tool for Total Quality Management*. Quality Press (1993), p. 48.
7. Bukkyo Dendo Kyokai. *The Teaching of Buddha*, 202nd revised edition. Society for the Promotion of Buddhism (1966), p. 54.
8. Said Boukendour and Daniel Brissaud. "A Phenomenological Taxonomy for Systemizing Knowledge on Nonconformances," *Quality Management Journal*, Vol. 12, No. 2, (2005).
9. Carter, Rita. *Mapping the Mind*. University of California Press (1998), p. 106.
10. Antonio R. Damasio. *Descartes' Error*. New York: Grosset & Putnam (1994).
11. Richard M. Restak. Receptors. New York: Bantam Books (1994). Robert Ornstein and Richard F. Thompson. *The Amazing Brain*. Boston: Houghton Mifflin (1984).
12. Vernon J. Bourke. *The Pocket Aquinas*. Washington Square Press. (1960), p. 67.

2

Conventional Wisdom Compared

Ignorance is a most wonderful thing. It facilitates magic. It allows the masses to be led. It provides answers when there are none. It allows happiness in the presence of danger.
All this, while the pursuit of knowledge can only destroy the illusion. Is it any wonder that humanity chooses ignorance?

— Dean L. Gano

Conventional wisdom in most subjects is nearly always wrong, but when coupled with the intellectual laziness and resistance to change inherent in the human condition, conventional wisdom leads to stasis and a dedication to ignorance. Such is the case with human problem solving. This chapter provides a short description and evaluation of the current and most common root cause analysis tools used in businesses throughout the world.

Now that we understand the fundamental problems with conventional thinking and how it prevents effective problem solving, let's take a look at the various methods people have created to help them solve event-type problems and compare these methods to the RealityCharting process. Because there is no subject or discipline dedicated to effective problem solving in the educational world, businesses have taken it upon themselves to create their own problem-solving processes. These different methods are generally referred to as "root cause analysis," and there are many books available today that discuss these conventional tools and processes.

If you want a more in-depth discussion of these methods, reference 1 provides one of the better comparisons, but it was written before RealityCharting was created, so there is no reference to it there.

Comparison Criteria

If we are to properly evaluate the many so-called root cause analysis methods and tools, we need a standard to which they can be compared. It is generally agreed that the purpose of root cause analysis is to find effective solutions to our event-based problems such that they do not recur. Accordingly, an effective root cause analysis process should provide a clear understanding of exactly how the proposed solutions meet this goal.

To provide this assurance, I believe an effective process should meet the following six criteria.

1. Clearly define the problem and its significance to the problem owners.
2. Clearly delineate the known causal relationships that combined to cause the problem.
3. Clearly establish causal relationships between the root cause(s) and the defined problem.
4. Clearly present the evidence used to support the existence of identified causes.
5. Clearly explain how the solutions will prevent recurrence of the defined problem.
6. Clearly document criteria 1 through 5 so others can easily understand the logic of the analysis.

Note: It should be noted that there is value in all of the tools and methods discussed herein, as they all help us better understand our world. The question in this discussion is which one(s) should you use to find the most effective solutions?

Various RCA Methods and Tools in Use Today

As you will discover in this analysis, there is a clear distinction between a root cause analysis (RCA) method and a tool. A tool is distinguished by its limited use, while a method may involve many steps and processes and has wide usage. I have labeled each process as a (Tool) or (Method).

Events and Causal Factors Charting:

(Tool) A complicated process that first identifies a sequence of events and aligns the events with the conditions that caused them. These events and respective conditions are aligned along a time line. Events and conditions that have evidence are shown in solid lines but evidence is not listed; all other observations are shown in dashed lines. After this representation of the problem is complete, an assessment is made by "walking" the chart and asking if the problem would be different if the events or conditions were changed. This leads to identifying causal factors such as training not adequate, management less than adequate, or barrier failed, which are identified by evaluating a tree diagram (discussed below).

Change Analysis:

(Tool) A six-step process that describes the event or problem, then describes the same situation without the problem, compares the two situations, and documents all the differences, analyzes the differences, and identifies the consequences of the differences. The results of the change analysis identifies the cause of the change and will frequently be tied to the passage of time and, therefore, easily fits into an events and causal factors chart, showing when and what existed before, during, and after the change. Change analysis is nearly always used in conjunction with another RCA method to provide a specific cause, not necessarily a root cause.

Barrier Analysis:

(Tool) An incident analysis that identifies barriers used to protect a target from harm and analyzes the event to see if the barriers held, failed, or were compromised in some way by tracing the path of the threat from the harmful action to the target. A simple example is a knife in a sheath.

The knife is the threat, the sheath is the barrier, and the target is a human. If the sheath somehow fails and a human is injured, the barrier analysis would seek to find out why the barrier failed. The cause of this failure is then identified as the root cause.

Tree Diagrams:

(Method) This type of root cause analysis is very common and goes by many names[1] such as Ishikawa Fishbone Diagram, Management Oversight and Risk Tree Analysis (MORT), Human Performance Evaluations System (HPES), and many other commercial brands. These methods use a predefined list of causal factors arranged like a fault tree (see Figure 2.1).

They are sometimes called "Pre-Defined Fault Trees." The American Society for Quality (ASQ) and others often call these categorical methods "Cause-and-Effect Diagrams." All categorization methods use the same basic logic. The premise is that every problem has causes that lie within a predefined set of categories. Ishikawa uses manpower, methods, machinery and environment as the top-level categories. Each of these categories has subcategories and sub-subcategories. For example, within the category of manpower, we may find management systems; within management systems we may find training; and within training we may find training less than adequate; and so on. These methods ask you to focus on one of the categories such as people and, in reviewing what you know of your event, to choose some causal factors from the predefined list provided. Each categorical method has its own list of causal factors.

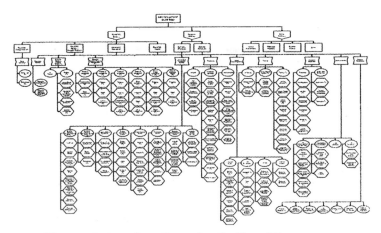

Figure 2.1. One Branch of a Tree Diagram

After reviewing the list for each category, you are asked to vote on which causal factors most likely caused your problem. After some discussion, the most likely ones are voted on and called "root causes." Solutions are then applied to these root causes to prevent recurrence. Each commercial brand of categorical method systems has a different definition of root cause, but it is generally a cause that you are going to attach a solution to that prevents recurrence. Some of these methods refer to themselves as "Expert Systems" and also provide predefined solutions for your problems.

Why-Why Chart:

(Method) One of many brainstorming methods also known as "the Five Whys method." This is the most simplistic root cause analysis process and involves repeatedly asking why at least five times or until you can no longer answer the question. Five is an arbitrary figure. The theory is that after asking why five times you will probably arrive at the root cause. The root cause has been identified when asking why doesn't provide any more useful information. This method produces a linear set of causal relationships and uses the experience of the problem owner to determine the root cause and corresponding solutions.

Pareto Analysis:

(Tool) A statistical approach to problem solving that uses a database of problems to identify the number of predefined causal factors that have occurred in your business or system. It is based on the Pareto principle, also known as the 80-20 rule, which presumes that 80% of your problems are caused by 20% of the causes. It is intended to direct resources toward the most common causes. Often misused as an RCA method, Pareto analysis is best used as a tool for determining where you should start your analysis.

Storytelling Method:

(Method) This is not really a root cause analysis *method* but is often passed off as one, so it is included for completeness. It is the single most common incident investigation method and is used by nearly every business and government entity. It typically uses predefined forms that include problem definition, a description of the event, who made a mistake, and what is going to be done to prevent recurrence. There is often a short list of root causes to choose from so a Pareto chart can be created to show where most problems originate.

Fault Tree Analysis:

(Method) Fault tree analysis (FTA) is a quantitative causal diagram used to identify possible failures in a system. It is a common engineering tool used in the design stages of a project and works well to identify possible causal relationships. It requires the use of specific data regarding known failure rates of components. Causal relationships can be identified with "and" and "or" relationships or various combinations thereof. FTA does not function well as a root cause analysis method, but is often used to support an RCA. More about this later.

Failure Modes and Effect Analysis:

(Tool) Failure modes and effects analysis (FMEA) is similar to fault tree analysis in that it is primarily used in the design of engineered systems rather than root cause analysis. Like the name implies, it identifies a component, subjectively lists all the possible failures (modes) that could happen, and then makes an assessment of the consequences (effect) of each failure. Sometimes a relative score is given to how critical the failure mode is to the operability of the system or component. This is called FMECA, where C stands for criticality.

RealityCharting:

(Method) A simple causal process whereby one asks why of a defined problem, answers with at least two causes in the form of an action and condition, then asks why of each answer and continues asking why of each stated cause until there are no more answers. At that time, a search for the unknown is launched and the process is repeated several times until a complete cause-and-effect chart, called a Realitychart, is created, showing all the known causes and their interrelationships. Every cause on the chart has evidence to support its existence or a "?" is used to reflect an unknown and thus a risk. All causes are then examined to find a way to change them with a solution that is within your control, prevents recurrence, meets your goals and objectives, and does not cause other problems. The result is clear causal connections between your solutions and the defined problem. Because all stakeholders can insert their causal relationships into the Realitychart, buy-in of the solutions is readily attained.

RCA Methods and Tools Compared

Many purveyors of root cause analysis state the process is so complicated that you should use several of them for each problem or select them based on which type of problem you are experiencing. In researching the various proponents of this approach, I find that the reason some people think root cause analysis is so complicated is that they don't understand the cause-and-effect principle. To quote Albert Einstein, "If you can't say it simply, you probably don't understand it."

Using the comparison criteria we established earlier, Figure 2.2. provides a summary of how each method or tool meets the criteria. One point is scored for each criterion that is met. "Limited" is scored as 0.5 points.

While the comparison in Figure 2.2 serves to show how poorly these conventional tools and methods provide effective solutions, it does not tell the whole story, as explained below.

Method/Tool	Type	Defines Problem	Defines All Known Causes	Provides A Causal Path To Root Causes	Delineates Evidence	Explains How Solutions Prevent Recurrence	Easy To Follow Report	Score
Events & Causal Factors	Method	Yes	Limited	No	No	No	No	1.5
Change Analysis	Tool	Yes	No	No	No	No	No	1
Barrier Analysis	Tool	Yes	No	No	No	No	No	1
Tree Diagrams	Method	Yes	No	No	No	No	No	1
Why-Why Chart	Method	Yes	No	Yes	No	No	No	2
Pareto	Tool	Yes	No	No	No	No	No	1
Storytelling	Method	Limited	No	No	No	No	No	0.5
Fault Tree	Method	Yes	Yes	Yes	No	Yes	No	4
FMEA	Tool	Yes	No	Limited	No	Limited	No	2
RealityCharting®	Method	Yes	Yes	Yes	Yes	Yes	Yes	6

Figure 2.2. Comparison of Selected RCA Methods and Tools

Events and Causal Factor Charting can provide the time line to help discover the action causes, but is generally inefficient and ineffective because it mixes storytelling with conditional causes, thus it produces complicated relationships that are not necessarily causal and this only serves to add confusion rather than clarity. Instead of identifying the many causal relationships of a given event, events and causal factor charting resorts to categorizing the important causes as causal factors, which are then evaluated as solution candidates using the same method as the categorization schemes discussed below. Events and Causal Factor Charting does not follow the principles of cause and effect discussed in chapter one.

Change Analysis is a very good tool to help determine specific causes or causal elements, but it does not provide a clear understanding of the causal relationships of a given event. Unfortunately, many people who use this method simply ask why the change occurred and fail to complete a comprehensive analysis.

Barrier Analysis can provide an excellent tool for determining where to start your root cause analysis, but it is not a method for finding effective solutions because it does not identify why a barrier failed or was missing. This is beyond the scope of the barrier analysis. To determine root causes, the findings of the barrier analysis must be fed into a principle based method to discover why the barrier failed.

Tree Diagrams also known as **Categorization Schemes**, are steadily being replaced with RealityCharting® but continue to retain a few followers because they appeal to our sense of order and "push-button" type thinking (as discussed in chapter one). There are at least seven major weaknesses in the tree diagram model.

Weakness 1. A tree diagram is clearly not a cause-and-effect chart, as the proponents of these methods would have us believe. It simply does not show all the causal relationships between the primary effect and the root causes. Consider the following example. Given a simple event, I have arranged the causes according to the rules of a fishbone diagram in Figure 2.3.

As we can see, the causal relationships are not clear at all. Could it be "Car Struck" was caused by "Foot on Accelerator" and "Truck Swerved" and "Truck Existed" and "Moving Truck?" Certainly these are some causes, but

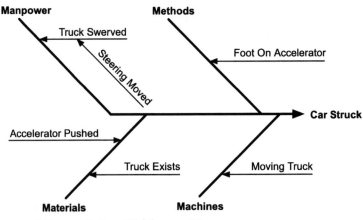

Figure 2.3. Fishbone Diagram

their relationships are not apparent. The diagram was created by looking at the event as I understand it, asking what causes could be classified as manpower, methods, materials, and machines and then placing those causes on the fishbone according to the categories they belong in—not how they are connected causally. The theory behind these tree diagrams is that because all events have certain causal factors we can find the root causes by looking for them in the predefined set provided. And while it can help jog the mind into certain lines of thinking, it fails to provide a causal understanding of the event. And without that understanding it is not possible to know if the causes you attach the solutions to will actually affect the defined problem.

If we use this same event and create a Realitychart (Figure 2.4) we can clearly see the causal relationships. I have added the categories to the top of each cause to emphasize how knowing the category provides no value whatsoever.

Weakness 2. No two categorization schemes are the same, nor can they be, because as discussed in chapter one, we each have a different way of perceiving the world.[2] Therefore, we have different categorical schemes and that is the reason there are so many different schemes being sold. When asked to categorize a given set of causes it is very

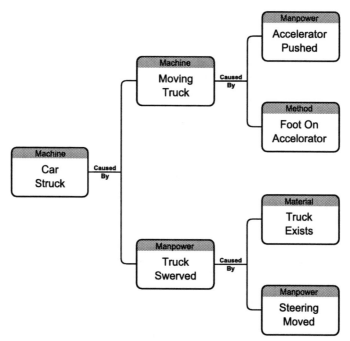

Figure 2.4. Realitychart vs. Categorization

difficult to find a consensus in any group. For example, what category does "Pushed Button" fall into? Some will see this as hardware; some will see it as people; and some will see it as procedure. If you have ever used any of these categorization methods to find a root cause, I know you have incurred many a wasted hour debating which is the correct category.

Weakness 3. The notion that anyone can create a list of causal factors that includes all the possible causes or causal factors of every human event should insult our intelligence. Ask yourself if your behavior can be categorized in a simple list and then ask if it is identical to every other human on the planet. The very fact that a method uses the term "causal factor" should be a heads-up that it does not provide a specific actionable cause but rather a broader categorical term representing many possible specific causes. At best, it acts as a checklist of possible causes for a given effect, but it does not provide any causal relationships. Since this error in logic is very contentious with those who use these methods, it begs the question why do these methods seem to work for them. What I have discovered, after talking with many people who claim success in using these methods, is that it works in spite of itself by providing some structure for the experienced investigator whose mind provides the actual causal relationships. It is not the methodology that works, but the experience of the investigator who is actually thinking causally. And while these methods seem to work for the experienced investigator, they are still incapable of communicating the reality of causal relationships. This inability to effectively communicate prevents the synergy among stakeholders necessary to fully understand the causes of the event, which is required to get buy-in for the solutions.

Weakness 4. These models do not provide a means of showing how we know that a cause exists. There is no evidence provided to support the causal factors in the list, so it is not uncommon for causal factors to be included that are politically inspired with no basis in fact. With these methods, the best storytellers or the boss often get what they want, and the problem repeats. This may help explain why many managers and self-proclaimed leaders like this method.

Weakness 5. Categorization schemes restrict thinking by causing the investigator to stop at the categorical cause. Some methods reinforce this fallacy by providing a "root cause dictionary," implying that it is a well-defined and recognized cause.

Weakness 6. Categorization methods perpetuate the root cause myth discussed in chapter one, based on the belief it is a root cause we seek and solutions are secondary. Because these methods do not identify complete causal relationships, it is not obvious which causes can be controlled to prevent recurrence; therefore, you are asked to guess and vote on which causal factors are the root causes. Only after root causes are chosen are you asked to identify solutions and without a clear understanding of all known causal relationships between the solution and the primary effect, this method works by chance not by design.

Weakness 7. As mentioned earlier, some of these categorical methods provide what is called an "expert system" and includes solutions for a given root cause. Expert systems can be quite useful for a very specific system such as a car or production line where most of the causal relationships are well known and have a long history of repeatability. To presume that one could provide an expert system applicable to all event-based problems seems to me to be incredibly arrogant. How could anyone presume to know the causal relationships for all systems, how they interrelate, and what constitutes the best solution for every organization or individual? Beware the salesperson.

As you can see from all these weaknesses Tree Diagrams are people centric and do not follow the principles of cause and effect discussed in chapter one.

The Five Whys method is inappropriate for any complicated event, but it is actually quite useful when used on minor problems that require nothing more than some basic discussion of the event. Unlike most of the other methods, it identifies causal relationships, but still subscribes to the root cause myth of first finding the root cause and then assigning solutions. It should never be used for formal incident investigations, but is perfectly acceptable for informal discussions of cause. A better approach to simple problems is RealityCharting Simplified™, a free software application that follows the Five Whys philosophy, but includes principle-based causal logic. To learn more about RealityCharting Simplified™ go to http://www.RealityCharting.com/RealityCharting/simplified.

Pareto Analysis uses a failure database to trend the frequency of categorical failures. This process is fraught with many landmines, a few of which are discussed below.

1. The accuracy of a Pareto chart is limited by the accuracy of the data used to create it. If you use a failed approach like tree

diagrams to determine the causes, the Pareto chart will only reflect causes from the predefined list provided.

2. The cause-and-effect principle dictates that all causes and effects are part of the same continuum. It many cases, certain causes will be closely linked (i.e., close to each other). For example, the cause "procedures not followed" could be caused by "procedures not accurate." In the Pareto analysis, this causal connection is lost. Instead, we see both "procedures not followed" and "procedures not accurate" in those top causes, so we end up working on solving both problems when in reality we may only need to solve the "procedures not accurate" problem. In this example, the incomplete view of reality provided by a Pareto analysis may have caused you to expend more resources than necessary.

3. Pareto analysis can mask larger, more systemic issues. For example, if quality management has transitioned into a state of dysfunction, this can cause symptoms in many different areas, such as poor procedures, inadequate resources, outdated methods, high failure rates, low morale, etc. Pareto analysis has you capturing all these symptoms of a larger problem as causes, and wasting time solving the symptoms rather than the problem.

Storytelling:

Perhaps the most common of all methods is storytelling, also known as the fill-out-a-form method. This method was discussed in more detail in chapter one but is summarized here for consistency. The primary difficulty with this approach is that you are relying completely on the experience and judgment of the report authors in assuring that the recommended solutions connect to the causes of the problems. The precise mapping between the problem and the recommended solutions is not provided.

The primary purpose of this method is to document the investigation and corrective actions. These forms usually do a good job of capturing the what, when, and where of the event, but little or no analysis occurs. Consequently, the corrective actions fail to prevent recurrence most of the time.

With such poor results, you might be wondering why organizations continue to use this method. The answer is twofold. First, most organizations do not measure the effectiveness of their corrective actions, so they don't know they are ineffective. Second, there is a false belief that everyone is a good problem solver, and all they need to do is document it on a form. For those organizations that recognize they are having repeat events, a more detailed form is often created that forces the users to follow a specified line of questions with the belief that an effective solution will emerge.

This is a false promise because the human thinking process cannot be reduced to a form. In our attempt to standardize the thinking process, we restrict our thinking to a predefined set of causes and solutions. The form tacitly signals the user to turn off the mind, fill in the blanks, and check the boxes. Because effective problem solving has been short circuited, the reports are incomplete and the problems keep occurring.

Fault Tree Analysis is not normally used as a root cause analysis method[3], primarily because it does not work well when human actions are inserted as a cause. This is because the wide variance of possible human failure rates prevents accurate results. But it works extremely well at defining engineered systems and can be used to supplement an RCA in the following ways:

1.   finding causes by reviewing the assumptions and design decisions made during the system's original design
2.   determining if certain causal scenarios are probable, and
3.   selecting the appropriate solution(s).

Additional insight into the various RCA methods, and how RCA integrates with quantitative methods such as fault tree analysis can be found in Reference 3.

To view this reference go to http://coach.realitycharting.com/_public/site/files/learning_center_libr/RCA-and-Quantitative-Methods.pdf.

Failure Modes and Effect Analysis:

Failure modes and effects analysis (FMEA) is sometimes used to find the cause of a component failure. Like many of the other tools discussed herein, it can be used to help you find a causal element within a Realitychart. However, it does not work well on systems or complex problems because it cannot show evidence-based causal relationships beyond the specific failure mode being analyzed.

RealityCharting:

RealityCharting is unlike all other RCA tools and methods. It is the only one that actually provides a graphical representation with evidence of all causes and their interrelationships. With this clear understanding of your reality, it can easily be communicated to other stakeholders, which allows them to add their reality, and in turn fosters a full appreciation of how the solutions will prevent the problem from recurring.

Summary

While conventional root cause analysis tools provide some structure to the process of human event-type problem solving, this review shows how they are significantly limited and often work by chance not by design. The common processes of storytelling and categorization are the product of thousands of years of evolution in our thinking, but it is time to move on. RealityCharting® is becoming the standard for all event analysis because it is the only process that understands and follows the cause-and-effect principles, thus it is the only process that allows all stakeholders to create a clear and common reality to promote effective solutions every time.

References

1. Paul Wilson, et al. *Root Cause Analysis—A Tool for Total Quality Management*. Milwaukee, WI: Quality Press (1993).
2. Paul M. Churchland. *The Engine of Reason, the Seat of the Soul*. Cambridge, MA: MIT Press (1996).
3. Larry Reising and Brett Portwood. 2007, "Root Cause Analysis and Quantitative Methods—Yin and Yang?" Presented at the International System Safety Conference (2007).

3

Understanding the Cause-and-Effect Principles

Things don't just happen; they are caused to happen.

—John F. Kennedy

Nothing happens without a cause. The notion of cause and effect is fundamental to all philosophies and major religions and still we hold to the whimsical adage that "stuff just happens." Highly effective problem solvers understand that there is no such thing as magic; there are only cause and effect and the unknown.

Cause-and-effect relationships govern everything that happens and as such are the path to effective problem solving. By knowing the causes, we can find some that are within our control and then change or modify them to meet our goals and objectives.

For at least 4,500 years, humankind has used the notion of causation to express human events.[1] Unfortunately, we have failed to differentiate the immense power of the cause-and-effect principle from the simple notion of causation. This chapter will take you on a journey into the depths of causation like never before documented. As we pull back the veil, we see four cause-and-effect principles:

- *Cause and effect are the same thing.*
- *Each effect has at least two causes in the form of actions and conditions.*
- *Causes and effects are part of an infinite continuum of causes.*
- *An effect exists only if its causes exist in the same space and time frame.*

We will examine each of these principles in detail so that we can build a set of tools that uses these principles to understand and document reality in a totally new way of thinking.

After teaching a class in a small town in Georgia, I was eating dinner one evening at a local restaurant. Sitting alone, I was busy watching people. A young family and their friends were seated at the table next to me. They had a small, perhaps nine-month-old, daughter seated in a highchair near her father. As the adults talked, the child was experimenting with a spoon. She banged it on the top of her highchair, licked it, and banged some more. In time, she leaned over the side of her chair and holding the spoon at arm's length, let it go. As it fell to the floor and bounced, she was immediately amazed. She looked around at the adults to see if they had seen this incredible event. They, of course, had missed it. In fact, she noticed they were paying no attention to her incredible discoveries. "What was the matter with them?" I read on her face.

With an outstretched arm and a grimace on her face, she reached for the spoon to no avail. After a few grunts and wanting cries, her father noticed her and returned the spoon to her tabletop. She smiled and returned to her play. After a few bangs, she decided to try the spoon drop experiment again. Again, it dropped straight down. It did not float upward like those big round colored objects she sometimes played with; this thing went straight down and bounced on the floor. Again, her face said it all. "This is really cool! Did you guys see that?" Looking up for acknowledgment, she seemed amazed at their total disregard for the profundity of her experiments. Again, she motioned and cried for the return of her object so she could further test the limits of her understanding. As the evening continued, she pestered her parents for the fallen spoon and proved that solid objects when released at height will always fall to the floor—it didn't matter if it was a spoon or mashed potatoes, stuff always went in the same direction.

As I watched this simple event, I saw a child learn about the law of gravity—but there was much more going on here. She was practicing a more fundamental life strategy. She was using her ability to control things and people to advance her understanding of the world.

And isn't this what we all do? We control things and we control people to accomplish our goals. In a moment of clarity, I realized that controlling causes is one of our most basic operating strategies. In the process of learning, we identify causal relationships (such as, things always fall down) and by controlling certain causes we are able to accomplish our goals. We learn that to obtain a desired effect we can act upon an object or person, and the effect will be caused to happen. Like the little girl, we may learn that if we whine enough, somebody will fill our need. The more specific knowledge we have about cause-and-effect relationships, coupled with our ability to act upon the causes within the relationships, the better our problem-solving skills. No matter how complex the causal relationships, be they mere feelings or hard scientific facts, the problem-solving process is always the same—understand the causal relationships, determine which ones you have control of, and act on them in a manner that meets your goals.

In the past, scholars tried to understand causation by labeling and categorizing different kinds of causes. Attorneys use proximate cause and probable cause. Safety engineers use surface causes, causal factors, apparent causes, and root causes. Aristotle had his four causes—efficient, material, formal, and final, which make no sense at all in today's world. By categorizing we create boundaries or boxes that define the category based on our own belief system. Because we all have different belief systems, categorization models immediately set up a quarrelsome environment. To avoid this, it is my goal here to discuss the principles of cause and effect without categorizing different types other than what is required to understand the principles of causation.

So, what is a cause and what is an effect, but more importantly, what is their relationship to reality? This simple notion of cause and effect is easy enough to grasp as the child did in the spoon drop experiment. However, as we will discover herein, there is much more to this fundamental idea than has ever been explained. Let's look at the four principles of causation so that we can understand their structure and how they present themselves.

Cause-and-Effect Principium

The cause-and-effect principium includes four principles:

1. Cause and effect are the same thing.
2. Each effect has at least two causes in the form of actions and conditions.
3. Causes and effects are part of an infinite continuum of causes.
4. An effect exists only if its causes exist in the same space and time frame.

Cause and Effect Are the Same Thing

When we look closely at causes and effects, we see that a "cause" and an "effect" are the same thing, or as others have stated, a single thing may be both a cause and an effect. They differ only by how we perceive them in time. When we start with an effect and ask why it occurred, we find a cause; but if we ask why again, what was just now a cause becomes

Effects		Causes
Injury	Caused By	Fall
Fall	Caused By	Slipped
Slipped	Caused By	Wet Surface
Wet Surface	Caused By	Leaky Valve
Leaky Valve	Caused By	Seal Failure
Seal Failure	Caused By	Not Maintained

Figure 3.1. Injury Example

an effect. This is shown in Figure 3.1 by listing a column of effects and a column of causes (read left to right, top to bottom).

Notice how the cause of one thing becomes the effect when you ask why again. The cause of the "Injury" was a "Fall," and when you ask why "Fall," it changes to an effect and the cause is "Slipped." This relationship continues as long as we continue to ask why.

When asking why of any given effect, we may not always agree on the answer because everyone has their own perspective. Others may perceive a cause or effect differently or more deeply if they have a greater understanding of the causal relationships. For example, we know we have a cold when we ache and cough, whereas a doctor knows we have a cold when he or she can observe a virus on a microscope slide. The effect is the same, but the knowledge of the causes is significantly different depending on perception and knowledge.

Knowing that cause and effect are the same thing only viewed from a different perspective in time helps us understand one reason why people can look at the same situation and see different problems. They are actually perceiving different time segments of the same event. If we treat each perspective as a different piece of a jigsaw puzzle, we can stop the usual arguing and work on putting the different pieces together.

By understanding that a cause and an effect are the same thing only from a different perspective, we get a glimpse of the next principle.

To help better understand this principle, go to http://coach. RealityCharting.com/Book/Exercise3.1.

Each Effect Has at Least Two Causes in the Form of Actions and Conditions

Causes are not part of a linear chain as depicted earlier, but more like a fishnet. As Figure 3.2 shows, we begin to see that each effect has two or more causes and the causes come in the form of conditions and actions.

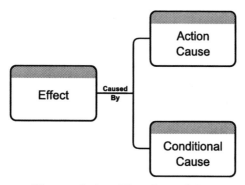

Figure 3.2. The Causal Set

That is, some causes (conditions) exist as a condition prior to the effect, while other causes (actions) seem to be in motion or otherwise active. The fundamental element of all that happens is a single causal relationship made up of an effect that is caused by at least one conditional cause, and at least one action cause.

Definitions

> **Actions** are causes that interact with conditions to cause an effect.
> **Conditions** are causes that exist in time prior to an action bringing
>   them together to cause an effect.
> **Causal set** is the fundamental causal element of all that happens. It
>   is made up of an effect and its immediate causes that represent
>   a single causal relationship. As a minimum, the causes consist of
>   an action and one or more conditions. Causal sets, like causes,
>   cannot exist alone. They are part of a continuum of causes with
>   no beginning or end.

It should be noted that conditions, while generally static or passive, may be in a state of motion and very short lived, such as a knee being at high speed. For example, the condition of knee at high speed, when combined with an action of impacted floor, results in the effect of kneecap broken.

By understanding this principle, we know we should look for two or more causes each time we ask why. Actions are the causes we most easily recognize, while conditions are often ignored. If we are able to see the conditions, we often find that several conditions come together with an action to cause some effect, as in the case of fire in the example of Figure 3.3.

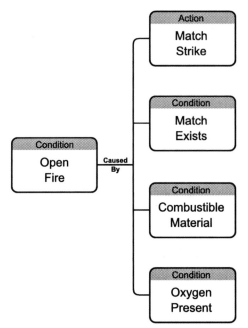

Figure 3.3.   Example of Conditions and Actions

As we ask "Why Open Fire?" we see that three conditions exist in the form of "Match Exists," "Combustible Material," and "Oxygen Present." The fire is created at the moment the match strike occurs. In this example, a match strike is the action; and as soon as that match strikes, we have a fire. It takes all three conditions and one action to create the fire.

To learn more about this principle go to http://coach.RealityCharting. com/Book/Exercise3.3.

Causes and Effects Are Part of an Infinite Continuum of Causes

As we observe the structure of the cause chain created by asking why, we are drawn to a linear path of causes. The causes presented in Figure 3.1 have been rearranged in Figure 3.4 to represent a linear chain of causes. This chain of causes seems to go on as long as we keep asking why and getting answers, so where does it start and where does it end?

In event-based problem solving, we always start with an effect of consequence that we want to keep from recurring and end at our point of ignorance. Our point of ignorance is where we can honestly admit we don't know why.

Presented with a reality that has a never-ending set of causes is something we have great difficulty accepting and probably explains why

Figure 3.4. A Continuum of Causes

we stop asking why at an early age and pursue simpler strategies like categorization and storytelling. Designed to find the right answer, the human mind simply cannot deal with not knowing[2] so we create answers when there are none. This is particularly true in group settings because we don't want to be embarrassed.[3]

Where we begin is a function of our own perspective. If we are the person responsible for valve maintenance in this example, we may choose to start asking why with the leaky valve or possibly the seal failure. If we were the safety engineer, our primary interest would be in preventing the injury from happening again, so we would probably start with injury and begin asking why.

What if we were the injured person? Our interest may be the pain, so our focus would start before "injury" at the effect of "pain"; and we would have a chain of causes that starts with "pain," as shown in Figure 3.5.

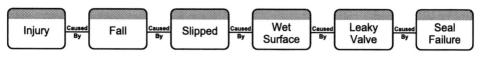

Figure 3.5. New Continuum of Causes

For our convenience, we are going to call this starting point the "primary effect."

A primary effect is any effect that we want to prevent from occurring and it can exist anywhere in the cause continuum.

The primary effect is not a universal point that we must somehow discover. It is a point in the cause chain where we choose to focus and begin asking why. This point can be changed anytime we need to change our focus. We may have more than one primary effect for a given event, which will be discussed later.

Knowing that causes and effects are part of an infinite continuum of causes helps us understand that, no matter where we start our problem analysis, we are always in the middle of a chain of causes. This helps us understand that there is no right place to start. Like a jigsaw puzzle, we can start the problem-solving process anywhere and still end up with a complete picture. This avoids the usual arguments over who is right and allows us to focus on finding causes. Instead of arguing over what the problem is, like we normally do, we can know that all causes are connected somehow in time and we just need to figure out the relationships.

But as we learned from the second principle, causes are not linear. They branch into at least two causes each time we ask why of an effect. As we begin to explore the possibilities, we begin to see that causes are part of an ever-expanding infinite set. Figure 3.6 shows what happens each time we ask why—we get an ever-expanding set of causes. If a fire has four causes and if each of those causes has four causes, then we can see that the total set of causes grows exponentially to infinite proportions.

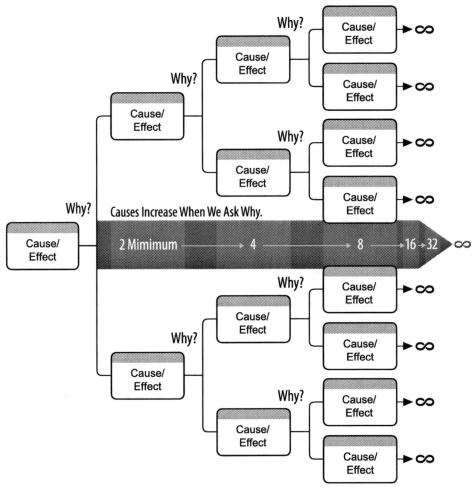

Figure 3.6.   Infinite Set of Causes

As we look at this ever-expanding set of causes, we are immediately overwhelmed with too much information and the mind cannot handle it.

The reason we don't see the infinite set of causes in our world is because we have learned to filter out most of the causes. We do this quite naturally by assigning priorities and focusing on certain cause paths. We discriminate by allowing only certain causes to be recognized in our conscious mind. The infinite set is there nonetheless. In fact, you could say that it defines reality, but we only see parts of it because we are limited by our knowledge, lack of interest, available time, and favorite solutions; the natural limitations of our minds and our language do not allow us to see it. And all these filters stifle the questioning attitude we were born with.

If we examine each of these limitations, we see that our level of knowledge limits our ability to know many causes. For example, if we were to ask "why gravity," our ignorance prevents an answer and therefore we cannot continue down this cause path. We must stop and say, "I don't know."

Our level of interest also determines our ability to know causes. In the fire example, where oxygen was listed as a cause, we may ask "why oxygen," but we don't because we are met with the immediate response of "who cares?" We know that this condition cannot be controlled in this situation and hence it has no value to us.

Lack of time keeps us from exploring every causal path in day-to-day problems. We limit our time according to our sense of value or our desire to pursue the problem. This leads to a strategy of checking past experiences to see if we have encountered the same problem before. If we have, we tend to search for the solutions that worked before and implement them. Quite often, we do not clearly identify the problem or spend time understanding the causes. We simply identify the problem categorically, such as human error, and impose our favorite solution, such as punishment or retraining.

Physical limitations of the mind restrict our ability to hold very many thoughts or ideas at the same time. George Miller, in a 1956 article in *Psychological Review*, first showed that adults could only hold about seven pieces of information (data) in the conscious mind at the same time. The variability of this number being plus or minus two. For example, we can usually add a few numbers together in our minds without resorting to pencil and paper: 46 + 54 = 100. Likewise, it is fairly easy to remember a seven-digit phone number, but a ten-digit long-distance number or adding several three-digit numbers usually brings out the pencil. Our conscious mental capacity is limited to a small number of thoughts, and yet we attempt to solve incredibly complex issues without writing them down. In the process we fail to express details and key pieces of information.

This ability to handle only seven, plus or minus two pieces of data may explain why some people believe the root cause appears after asking five whys. Although we have incredible storage capacity, our working memory and current conscious thinking are very limited.

With this severe limitation and the problems language presents (more on this later), we need some kind of tool or language aid to help keep our thoughts in front of us. This tool would have to allow an infinite set of ideas to be represented. It would have to be clear and simple to use. If we could develop this tool for problem solving and somehow identify all the causes of an event, we could use it to help decide how best to solve our more complex problems. Prior to RealityCharting® this tool never existed.

It is important to remember that while our minds naturally filter out or never know many of the causes of a problem, the causes are there nonetheless. Perhaps the single biggest lesson I have learned from all my studies of human problem solving it is that we must be humble above all things, because the only thing I am sure of is that in the face of the infinite set of causes, we really don't have the slightest idea what is going on.

This principle helps us understand the old saying that the more we know, the more we know we don't know. As you can see from this basic causal structure, every time we ask why we get at least two answers, and at some point along each cause path, we come to our point of ignorance, where we no longer have answers, but because of this principle, we know there must be at least two more causes—we just don't know what they are.

To learn more, go to http://coach.RealityCharting.com/Book/ Exercise3.6.

An Effect Exists Only if Its Causes Exist in the Same Space and Time Frame

Cause-and-effect relationships exist with or without the human mind, but we perceive them relative to time and space. From observation we see that an effect exists only if its causes exist in the same space and time frame. For example, the little girl's spoon fell because of at least three causes: gravity, the condition of holding the spoon at some height, and her action of letting it go. If these causes did not exist at the same time frame and space, the spoon would not fall. If the spoon is on the floor, it is in a different space and cannot fall; or if the girl never let go, the spoon never would have fallen.

Every effect we observe in the physical world is caused by at least one action cause coming together with existing conditional causes in the same relative space. A causal relationship is made up of conditional causes with a history of existence over time combining with another cause in some defined time frame to create an effect. If we were able to see the world in stop-action, we could see, for example, a nail held in place by a hand and a hammer's head striking the nail to cause the effect of two boards being nailed together. The nail, hand, hammer, carpenter, strong arm, and wood all exist as conditional causes at the same relative place and in the same time frame of the swinging hammer striking the nail and driving it through the two boards.

One of the greatest difficulties in understanding this time-space relationship is the fact that we do not see our world in stop-action. The world we perceive is one continuous linear set of causes, all acting together like the frames of a motion picture. Our language even prevents us from expressing our thoughts in anything other than a linear time-based sequence. For example, inside the raging fire are many unseen causes coming and going at a rapid pace. If we step back and look at the big picture, we might see something different, as the following example demonstrates.

Since oxygen has existed on this planet for about 2.3 billion years and is always present in our atmosphere, we show it in Figure 3.7 as extending over a long period of time. The oily rags probably have existed only for a short period of time. Assuming the matches existed in the room near the rags for some shorter period of time, one of the matches is struck next to the rags, and we have the effect of a fire. We could say that actions are causes that bring conditions together, as long as we understand that "bring together" does not always imply physical movement. Conditions are causes that exist prior to an action and are required for the effect to occur. Like the ingredients of soup, each component is a condition; and it isn't soup until the cook says its soup. At that moment, the mixture becomes soup, until it is eaten.

When asking why of a primary effect, our linear thinking usually only provides one answer. However, as discussed, every effect is created by at least two causes (conditional and action) coming together. These conditional and action causes must each have the same when and where associated with them for the effect to occur. If we do not see this time-space relationship, the causal relationship is not valid.

There is also a relative time frame component to the causal element. For the example above we represent the match strike as instantaneous. However, if our primary effect is something like "Road Exists," caused by

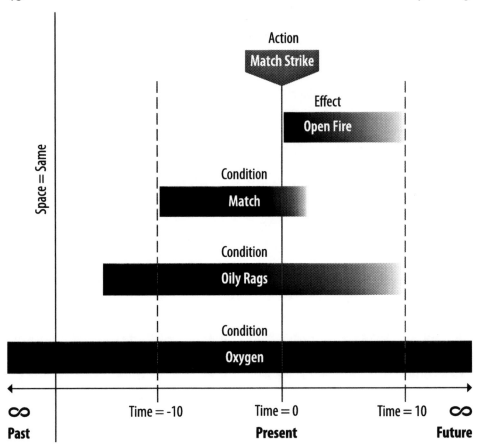

Figure 3.7.   Fire Example as a Function of Time

"Road Constructed (Action)" + "Asphalt Exists (Condition)" + "Manpower (Condition)," etc., the time frame for the action cause is much longer than the action cause of the fire. See Figure 3.8.

What makes the causes valid for a given causal element is that all the causes in that element exist *at the same time frame*, where the time frame is relative to the stated causes. What becomes obvious after this discussion is that it is not easy to communicate these simple concepts because everything is relative, and our minds have difficulty processing more than one relative concept at a time, which in turn is reflected in our language. All modern languages propel us along a linear time line from past to present. They do not allow for branches of conditions and actions. I suspect that if we thought this way, language would have developed to allow discussion of the infinite set of causes, but we are really very primitive creatures and like to keep things simple. Even the

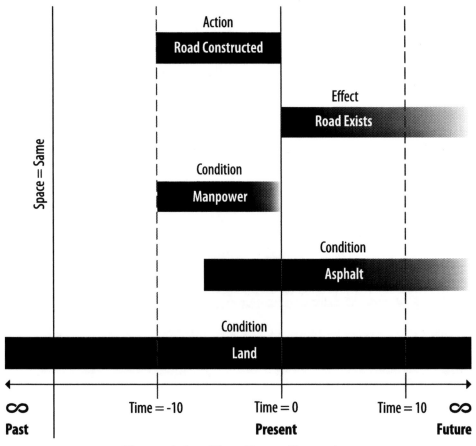

Figure 3.8. Time Frame Example

notion of infinity is difficult for most people, so it is understandable that our language reflects a simple linear causal-thinking pattern without conditional and action branches.

To have some fun with this principle, go to http://coach. RealityCharting.com/Book/Exercise3.7.

Inside the Cause-and-Effect Principle: Baby Steps

If we look inside the dynamics of causal relationships, we begin to see that not only does the infinite continuum of causes expand along both ends of the time line and expand exponentially each time we ask why, but also that there are always causes between the causes. If we change the relative time frame of a causal element to a shorter time frame, we will see more detailed causes.

In our injury example of Figures 3.1 and 3.2, we said the cause of the injury was a fall. While this is a valid statement, there are several possible causes between injury and fall. The example in Figure 3.9 shows the causes between causes and the branches in the cause path. The closer we look and the more we ask why, the more causes we find between the causes. Realizing this begs the question: How far should we go when asking why? The simple answer is always go to your point of ignorance or until you

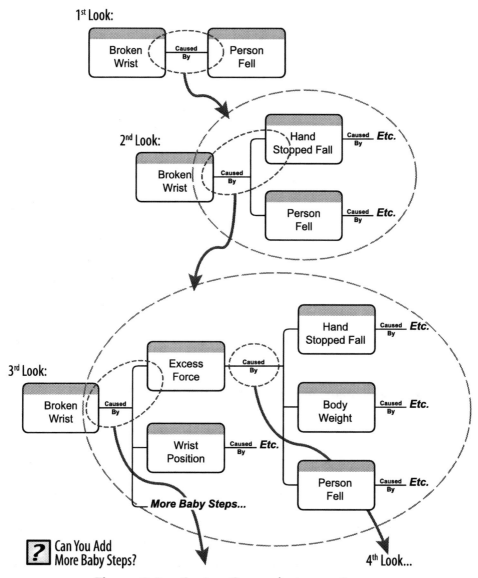

Figure 3.9. Seeing Causes between Causes

decide to stop. The decision to stop should be based on the significance of the problem and your ability to find the best solution.

The limitations of our ability to understand the infinite set of causes also apply to our inability to know all the causes between the causes. Every causal relationship can be broken into smaller and smaller pieces with each shortening of the reference time frame. I call these causes "baby-step causes" because they are like the baby steps we take in the process of learning to run. They are there but are forgotten or unknown to all observers.

Baby steps are found by looking between the causes, but they are often elusive. The more we ask why, the closer we get to understanding specific causal relationships; but the fact is, we will never know all of them. A good example of this is the use of antibiotics today. When first introduced, antibiotics could kill just about any bacterium we wanted eradicated. Today, some bacteria can only be controlled by one antibiotic, and scientists estimate that soon these bacteria will no longer be destroyed by any antibiotic.

When scientists first began using antibiotics, they developed a theoretical model of how a bacterium affects the body. After understanding most of the causal relationships, they found a way to control some of the causes so that the bacterium was killed inside the body. This produced the desired effect of returning to a healthy state, but other causes were acting as well. The bacteria are continually evolving and changing their genetic makeup as a result of environmental influences. Scientists continue to redefine their theoretical model; however, the fact remains, they do not understand all the causal relationships.

We often know enough about the causal relationships of a system to cause certain effects to exist, but we do not know all the causes. We must know more causes of cancer before we can hope to have an effective cure. When that day comes, our current methods will likely seem as barbaric as the bloodletting procedures from the past seem to us today.

When identifying causes, try to go to the level that provides the best understanding of the causal relationship. This can vary, depending upon our needs.

To help you internalize this concept, work the exercise at the following link: http://coach.RealityCharting.com/Book/Baby-Steps.

Linear Language, Linear Thinking

With a new appreciation for cause-and-effect relationships, let's take a deeper look at storytelling and language. Stories, our primary form of communication, conflict with the cause-and-effect principle in three ways:

1. Stories start in the past, while causal relationships start with the present.
2. Stories are linear, while causal relationships follow the branches of the infinite set.
3. Stories use inference to communicate meaning, while legitimate causal relationships require clear evidence of the existence of each cause.

Let's examine a simple story to see how detrimental these conflicts are.

The little handicapped boy lost control of the run-down wagon and it took off down the hill on a wild ride until it hit the little blind girl next to the drinking fountain by Mrs. Goodwin. The little boy was in the wagon the whole way but was not injured. The boy's mother should never have left him unsupervised. The root cause of the girl's injury was human error.

Stories Start in the Past

As you can see, the story starts in the past at the top of the hill and progresses through time from the past to the present, from the beginning of the ride to the end, from the safe condition to the stated problem of injury. The conflict this creates is that by going from past to present we do not see the branched causal relationships of actions and conditions. If we could know every cause of this injury example, we would see a diagram of cause-and-effect relationships similar to Figure 3.6. That is, we would see a set of ever-expanding causes starting with the injury and proceeding into the past. To express what we know causally in story format, we would first need to express all the causes on the right-hand side of the diagram, i.e., starting from the past. Our language and the rules of storytelling simply do not allow for this. We cannot express sixteen causes and then tell what they caused and so on. No one would sit still for a story told this way because stories are about people, places, and things as a linear function of time.

Stories Are Linear

As we look at this simple story, or any story, we find our language restricts us to a linear path through time and space. Stories go from A to B to C, linearly through time without regard for the order of causal relationships. We are told of the little boy losing control of the wagon as it goes down the hill and strikes the little blind girl. There is no ever-expanding set of branched causes expressed like those in Figure 3.6.

We have the ability to escape this linearity and express branches if we use the words "and" and "or," but the rules of grammar tell us not to use these connecting words excessively. The best we can accomplish is one or two branches for each sentence. The conflict arises because the cause-and-effect principle dictates an infinite set of causes for everything that happens, while stories are created and expressed linearly.

Storytelling, whether it is ancient history or a recent event description, is a linear understanding of an event in a time sequence from past to present, and totally ignores the cause-and-effect principle. Because we do not understand the branched causes of the infinite set, we use our own understanding of cause, which is generally to follow the action causes.[4] (See Reference 4, for an extensive discussion of this effect.) Because we typically fail to see conditions as causes, we ignore them and primarily focus on a linear set of action causes, which are often initiated by people.

Stories Use Inference to Communicate Causes

Since good stories seem to provide us with a valid perception of what happened, we need to question how this can occur in light of the above conflicts. The key word here is "perception." When we read or hear a story, our mind provides most of the information.[2] As we read the words, we are busy creating images in our mind's eye. These images are created from past experience and assembled into a sequence of events.

Because the sequence of events (the story) does not express the branched causes of the infinite set, we must make up for it somehow and we do this by inference. We infer causes within the story that are not stated. For example, we read that the little handicapped boy lost control of the wagon. Since no cause is stated for how he lost control, we can infer anything our mind will provide, and we do just that if questioned about it. Was the loss of control somehow caused by being handicapped? Could be, and many people might make that assumption, but it would be wrong.

Furthermore, stories infer cause by the use of prepositions such as "in," "on," "with," etc. Prepositions and conjunctions by definition infer a relationship between words, and the relationship is left to the reader. The word "and" is often used to mean "caused." In this story we read that the boy lost control of the wagon *and* it took off down the hill, meaning the loss of control caused the wagon to take off down the hill. Within this "and" is the potential for many causal relationships and they are left for the reader to interpret. For me, the "and" between *lost control* and *took off down the hill* is obviously a broken steering mechanism, while someone else may picture lack of control by a paraplegic little boy as the cause, and the next person sees the wagon wheel strike a rock that causes the wagon to veer sharply. Because we do not express what is happening causally, each word in the story provides the reader with the opportunity to know more about the event than is stated—to interpret the situation from his or her own biased mind, which is not necessarily what actually happened.

In the end, each one of us thinks we know what happened, but we really don't because stories do not express the full set of causal relationships. Our linear language and the linear thinking behind it prevent us from knowing and expressing what really happens in any given situation. Couple this with the notion of common sense and the false belief in a single reality and you have the causes for miscommunication and ineffective problem solving that is so prevalent in every human endeavor. You have the cause of why almost every decision-making meeting includes conflict and arguments.

What we need is some way to communicate and assemble the causal relationships that each one of us brings to the table. By breaking away from storytelling and knowing the causal set for the problem at hand, we can find effective solutions every time. Just imagine what would happen if politicians were required to create a Realitychart before they enacted laws to solve a problem.

The Cause-and-Effect Principle Defines Reality

By understanding the cause-and-effect principle, we now know the basic structure that reality must follow. Knowing this allows us to represent any situation using causes—all we have to do is fill in the blanks. By knowing that causes are part of an infinite continuum, we know that no matter where we start working on a problem we are always in the middle. Since cause and effect are the same thing, we can move forward or backward along the cause continuum as we learn more about the causal relationships of our problem. With this flexibility we eliminate the typical bickering about what the problem really is. All ideas are accepted and aligned causally in time from present to past.

By looking for an action cause and conditional causes of each effect, we gain a much clearer picture of the problem and its causes. By understanding the notion of an infinite set of causes, we are no longer restricted by our own paradigms. We know that each cause is like a piece of a puzzle and each person's perspective provides insight into the causes. With this understanding, the task becomes one of assembling all perspectives rather than bickering over who has the correct ones.

By understanding the four principles of the cause-and-effect principium, we can create tools that will help us break out of the old paradigms of linear and categorical thinking. These new tools will allow us to escape the death grip of a single reality and encourage everyone involved to share their ideas and thoughts. In doing so, everyone will come together with their own realities to form the common reality we need to be the best we can be. And being principle-based, this tool will work on any event-type problem.

To practice what you learned about using RealityCharting®, go to http://coach.RealityCharting.com/Book/Practice-Time.

References

1. Charles Van Doren. *A History of Knowledge*. New York: Ballantine Books (1991).
2. Rita Carter. *Mapping the Mind*. Los Angeles: University of California Press (1999).
3. Daniel Goleman. *Emotional Intelligence*. New York: Bantam Books (1995).
4. Fred. A. Manuele. *On the Practice of Safety*, second edition. New York: John Wiley & Sons (1997).

4

Step One: Define the Problem

A problem well stated is a problem half-solved.

—Charles Kettering

Defining the problem is the first step in the problem-solving process, so take the time to write it down before proceeding to the next step. A complete problem definition should include four elements:

- *What is the problem?*
- *When did it happen?*
- *Where did it happen?*
- *What is the significance of the problem?*

You will notice that the problem definition does not ask who or why. Who questions lead to placing blame and are generally a waste of time. Why questions are reserved for the analysis phase of problem solving.

The first step in the RealityCharting process is defining the problem. Let's look more closely at a typical business meeting where we have to decide how to resolve a pressing issue. The scenario goes something like this.

Boss: "Okay, I'm glad everyone could be here. As you know, we have experienced another [insert your problem here]. This is the third time this has happened in as many weeks. Now, we all know what's going on, so what I want to do here today is fix this thing once and for all. Does anyone have any ideas on how we can prevent this from happening again?"

As the boss makes the statement about everyone knowing what the problem is, many people are nodding their heads in agreement, giving him the positive feedback that they are in tune with his thinking. They may even smile at one another in agreement. The body language is ripe with consensus and the air is full of confidence, but problem definition is not discussed. The stated goal is preventing recurrence and solutions are solicited. Discussion ensues with expressed opinions and everyone is carefully listening to the boss to know which way to lean. Yet everyone sees and expresses the problem differently. Few, if any, of these team members will see the problem being within their domain. They will see the problem from their perspective, but their typical solution will be to have someone else change.

Figure 4.1.

The dynamics of these decision-making meetings are predictable, and the path is the same almost every time. When we look more closely, this is what happens.

First, the problem is not defined. It is assumed that everyone knows the problem. After all, it has happened at least three times, so everyone surely knows what it is by now. The assumption is that it is so obvious we need not waste time discussing it. This thinking is based on the illusion of common sense. In the meantime, every person in the meeting is thinking to themselves, "Yes, I know what the problem is—if the other manager would only get off the dime and do what I told him/her to do, this wouldn't be happening." Each person sees a piece of the puzzle based on their perspective, but none see the whole picture. Eventually, communication stops, the boss is left to make a decision, and no one is happy.

Second, there is no discussion of causes; or if there is, a few causes are expressed using storytelling. Any discussion about causes usually deteriorates into a debate won by the person who can tell the best story, usually the boss.

Third, the discussion is centered around possible solutions. We are so solution oriented, we ignore the causes and debate the solutions. The analysis phase of problem solving is essentially ignored because we mistake decision making for analysis. Managers especially slip into this trap. They listen to various stories and see their role as the decision maker, not the analyst. They use their "experience" as the basis for the decision when they should be using the known causal relationships.

Defining the problem should seem obvious to us, yet we fail to do this adequately about 95% of the time. Sure, we state something as being wrong or bad or unacceptable, but we don't stop and write it down or take the time to fully understand the significance of the problem. The act of writing down the what, when, where, and the significance of the problem provides focus. We fail to do this because the problem seems so obvious: the plant shutdown, or the lost-time injury, or the poor quality of service. These things have happened before so we don't need to define them, or so the misguided thinking goes.

Defining the problem is the first step in the problem-solving process, so take the time to do it adequately. The following discussion provides detailed guidance to help you be successful. In the RealityCharting process, getting the "right" problem definition the first time is not as critical as it is for other methods because, as you identify more causes, you may find that you started in the middle and need to redefine the problem. Quite often the problem is something bigger than you originally thought and you need to redefine it. This is very easy to do with the RealityCharting process, so don't waste a lot of time trying to make sure you have a perfect problem definition the first time.

Complete Problem Definition

A complete problem definition should include four elements:

■ *What* is the problem?
■ *When* did it happen?
■ *Where* did it happen?
■ What is the *significance* of the problem?

The what of any problem is the effect of consequence or the gap between an existing condition and a preferred state or condition. This is the effect we do not want to recur, and hence we are calling it the "primary effect." The primary effect is the beginning of asking why. It is a noun-verb statement such as "Clock Stopped," "Arm Broken," "System Failed," etc.

To learn more, go to http://coach.RealityCharting.com/Book/What.

The when of any problem may be a very specific point in time, but it can also be a relative time of the primary effect. It may be the time of day or the point in a sequence of causes, such as "during night shift."

To learn more, go to http://coach.RealityCharting.com/Book/When.

The where of any problem may be a very specific place, but it can also be a relative location of the primary effect. It may be the physical coordinates on a map, or a building, or the position relative to something else, such as "the swimming pool next to the tennis courts."

To learn more, go to http://coach.RealityCharting.com/Book/Where.

The significance of any problem is the relative value the primary effect has on you or your organization. It is the answer to the question, "Why are we working on this problem?"

Knowing the significance up front not only helps us prioritize the need to work on the problem, it also helps us determine which causes to pursue and which solutions are within our control. Significance can involve many factors, but the most common ones are cost, safety, and frequency.

Properly assessing the significance of the problem is perhaps the most important element of defining the problem. By knowing the significance in the initial problem definition phase, we determine the required effort and priority of the problem before proceeding; we may even determine not to pursue the problem at all.

If a problem resulted in the loss of business or a severe injury, the problem is significant and deserves attention. In personnel performance issues, frequency may determine our corrective action. If an employee who frequently makes mistakes caused a problem and our causes lead us to find he or she chooses not to learn, our corrective action legitimately could be to terminate employment. But, if the problem was caused by the lapse in concentration of a valued employee after twenty years of error-free work, the significance is radically different; and we may choose to do nothing for the exact same set of causes.

As another example, if a fall caused a broken wrist and the wrist is mine, the significance might be minimal if it happened once in thirty years of snow skiing because the frequency is acceptable to me. With this minimal significance, I may only need to understand a few causes to help me avoid the conditions that set me up to fail. If, on the other hand, the broken wrist was that of a professional football player, this was the third time it happened, and this same event kept him and three other players off the field for six weeks each, then the significance is much greater than my skiing injury. In this situation we may need to understand a hundred causes to find an effective solution. Each situation is different, and you will learn from experience how far to go to find the best solutions.

The greater the significance, the more important it may be to know the causes between the causes because each new cause adds more opportunities for an effective solution. Including the significance in the problem definition is essential to effective problem solving.

When stating the significance, be specific and try to avoid categorical statements. Instead of injury, the significance may be stated as "lost use of hand" or instead of "plant shut down," we should state "lost $50,000 in production costs."

Significance is relative to our goals and objectives. If our organization has a goal to produce something safely and economically or to provide the best service possible, the significance of the problem should center around these goals. Oftentimes organizations fail to communicate their goals and objectives to each employee. When employees do not know what their specific goals are, they find it difficult to identify the significance of a particular problem. The result is an incomplete problem definition and difficulty in determining an effective solution. The employees are often left trying to guess what the boss wants, rather than thinking for themselves to accomplish an important objective.

Knowing the significance also helps us know which questions to ask during the analysis phase. As we go down the various cause paths, knowing significance helps us decide which paths may provide the best solutions. For example, if my problem is a waste spill, then knowing what kind of waste it is not only tells me what the significance is, it also tells me which why questions to ask later. If it is just dirty water, then I may only need to find out why it got out of its container. If it is toxic waste, then I may need to ask more why questions to find out why it was not contained by a secondary containment system.

Significance is completely relative and unique to each problem, but if we don't define it up front, it has a tremendously negative impact on our ability to effectively and efficiently solve our problems.

To learn more, go to http://coach.RealityCharting.com/Book/ Significance.

To see how RealityCharting can help you define the problem, work the following exercises at this link: http://coach.RealityCharting.com/ Book/PD-Exercises.

What the Problem Definition Is Not

You will notice that the problem definition does not ask who or why. Who questions lead to placing blame and are generally a waste of time. Why questions are reserved for the analysis phase of problem solving.

The only acceptable who question is, "Who knows the answer to my other questions?" Unfortunately, "who?" is one of our most often asked questions, and we need to stop doing it. Asking "who?" is understandable, not only because we seek to know who caused the action but also because of a very personal human condition. Consider this: When we are presented with a failure of consequence that we feel personally responsible for, the very first question we ask ourselves is, "Did I screw up?" If the answer to this question is "no," we immediately and universally ask the next question: "Who did?"

If the answer is "yes, I screwed up," we either accept responsibility and try to learn from our mistake or more often seek to find a way to implicate other people or other things. If the answer is "maybe I screwed up," we seek to divert negative consequences by developing a rationale that points elsewhere: "The devil made me do it" or "The dog ate it."

The point is, we need to understand that this need to find a who is ingrained in our being and is therefore very difficult to stop. It must be a conscious effort. Asking someone to remind us of this tendency often works well because it keeps both people more conscious of the need.

In time it becomes a habit and we stop asking who; and when we catch others doing it, we remind them not to go there.

The why questions may be asked early in the problem-solving process. While this is not wrong, it can be inefficient. It should be held back until the problem is defined and written down. Because causes and effects are the same thing and we are seeking the primary effect in the what phase of the problem definition, we will inevitably get into causes during problem definition. However, asking why is the essence of the analysis phase and is a separate step unto itself. It is not that we have to define the problem and leave it, never to come back, but we need a place to start. By defining the problem, we define the starting point and can get on with asking why.

It is common to start with one primary effect only to realize that it is a symptom of a more significant problem and that we need to redefine the problem. As we discover the different perspectives of each contributing person (stakeholder), several elemental causal sets will be generated. They should be noted, but the focus should remain on finding the one effect that seems to stand out as the most significant one. The causal sets or individual causes should be documented for later discussion. A more detailed discussion of this is provided in chapter twelve.

Conflicting Goals

Defining the problem is usually very easy, but when many stakeholders are involved, such as public projects, a new dynamic presents itself and we need to be aware of it. The purpose of event-type problem solving is to move from the current unacceptable state or condition to a desired condition. Unfortunately, the desired condition is not always easily defined, especially when politics is involved. One stakeholder's goals may be different from another's or from those of an organization. Because goals define the purpose and purpose defines the significance and significance helps define the problem, conflicting goals will result in an impossible problem-solving environment.

For example, in the northwestern United States there is one political goal of saving the salmon in the rivers and the proposed solution is to remove all the hydroelectric dams on the Columbia and Snake Rivers. Another political goal is use the dams to provide a viable economy by providing carbon-free electricity for the region and irrigation water for farms to grow food. Unfortunately, the proponents of dam removal have supplanted their goal of saving the fish with a solution to remove the dams. Without any comprehensive causal analysis by anyone, they have determined that dam removal is the only solution to meet their goal. With this conclusion, they have changed their goal from "Restore salmon runs" to "Remove dams." They have moved from focusing on the undesired effect of decreased salmon population to a solution mindset that no longer incorporates causal relationships. Since this is in direct conflict with the goal of providing a viable economy and food to eat, the two entities have continued this losing battle for over thirty years and until such time as politicians realign their goals and do a comprehensive causal analysis, the folly will continue.

5

Step Two: Determine the Causal Relationships

We can evade reality, but we cannot evade the consequences of evading reality.

—Ayn Rand

Causal relationships are defined by the cause-and-effect principles discussed in chapter three. Understanding these principles allows us to put form to the structure of reality such that we can be more responsible for our success in life. In this chapter, we will move from principle to tool and define how to create the causal structure of an event.

Based on the cause-and-effect principles discussed in chapter three we are able to create a simple process that will allow us to establish a common reality from the diversity of thought in any organization.

This process is as follows:

1. For each primary effect, ask why.
2. Look for causes in actions and conditions.
3. Connect all causes with "Caused By" statements.
4. End each cause path with a question mark or a reason for stopping.

We start with the what that we identified in the initial problem definition. This is called the primary effect and is the point at which we begin asking why. As we answer the why questions, we identify the condition and action causes of the primary effect. By connecting all causes with the words "Caused By," the detrimental effects of storytelling are mitigated. The fourth step of the process prevents us from stopping too soon by forcing us to address why we stopped. These fundamental elements of the Realitychart are found in Figure 5.1.

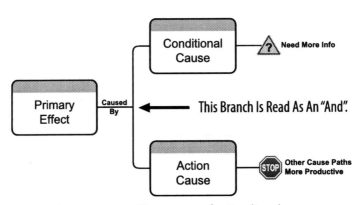

Figure 5.1.   Elements of a Realitychart

Where to Start

When starting the problem-solving process, there is usually not enough information to feel comfortable about the primary effect, so you may have several effects, in which case you may need several charts. But don't worry about bringing them together because RealityCharting® makes this very easy to do. Instead of arguing or wasting time trying to decide on one primary effect or starting point, list the primary effects you have and attack each one—one at a time, identifying as many known causes as you can. What is happening during this stage of the process is that each team member is expressing their own reality about what happened, and they often differ. People are expressing their perspectives of the event—no one is right or wrong, so focus on capturing these perspectives. We will sort them out later. The purpose of this process is to capture all causes and their relationships. You may want to have each stakeholder use RealityCharting Simplified™, to easily create a Realitychart of what they know. RealityCharting Simplified™ is a free software application that allows all stakeholders to answer some basic questions and in doing so, automatically creates a Realitychart. The file can be saved and emailed to a facilitator for incorporation into a master chart. For more information go to http://www.realitycharting.com/ RealityCharting/simplified.

If you are in a meeting-type setting and want to brainstorm causes to get started, RealityCharting® provides a brainstorming feature to help you. To see how this works, go to http://coach.RealityCharting.com/Book/ Brainstorming.

Creating a Realitychart is much like putting together a jigsaw puzzle—we start with one piece and try to find a match. We put together a few pieces at a time and then run out of connections, so we start with another piece and repeat the process. With each success we create an elemental causal set, which is a single causal relationship made up of at least one conditional cause and one action cause that caused the effect.

Eventually these elemental causal sets will combine to form a picture or common reality just like a jigsaw puzzle. If the pieces don't fit, they are probably part of another problem or are inconsequential data. The only significant difference between creating a jigsaw puzzle and a Realitychart is that the chart has no boundaries.

This concept of no boundaries is difficult to get used to because there is a strong sense that you have lost control. The fact is, you never were in control so don't let these feelings get to you! When nothing seems to fit together, keep reminding yourself of the jigsaw puzzle; it will always fit together if you have the perseverance to follow these strategies. Have faith in the process and, just like the jigsaw puzzle, with a little patience and tenacity, the picture will become clearer each time you repeat the steps.

When the Realitychart is finished, there is usually only one primary effect left. If you have some causes left over, chances are they are part of another problem, or you have chosen to separate different parts of the event.

The more complicated the event, the greater the chance of multiple primary effects. Remember, because of the cause-and-effect principle, all causes are connected with all other causes in some way. Trying to show these connections may make your understanding of the problem too complicated. If the problem is as big as an elephant, how should we eat the elephant? One bite at a time, of course. Eating it whole would be impossible, so we need to divide the problem into smaller parts by focusing on separate primary effects. We call this "chunking" and it allows each part of a problem to be assigned to different teams.

As we learned in chapter one, in the Deepwater Horizon Oil Well Incident, the investigators found eight key findings and four critical factors. Each one of these would be a good place to start a Realitychart. Figures 5.2 and 5.3 provide an example of this. As we continue to ask and answer the why questions, we will find more and more causes and the picture becomes clearer. Some of these Realitycharts will combine and others may not.

Figure 5.3 includes the critical factor of "Hydrocarbons Flowing" and the key finding that the "Shoe Track Failed." Instead of categorizing causes into critical factors and key findings like BP did, with this perspective we begin to see the causal relationships of the event and thus have a much better understanding of reality.

The shoe track is a device placed at the bottom of the well to facilitate isolation of the well from the high-pressure oil reservoir in the earth. At first glance, it seems a waste of time to list its existence as a cause because it is so obvious. As you will discover later, however, conditional causes may be the best ones to attach a solution to. If we ask why does the shoe track exist, we may be able to get outside our normal thinking and discover another way to isolate the well bottom. Perhaps there is a better way to do this and you certainly will not go to this level of questioning if you do not list the obvious conditional causes on the chart and challenge them.

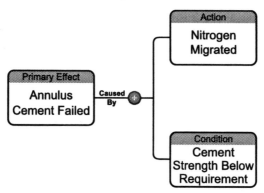

Figure 5.2. First Causal Element for Annulus Cement Failed

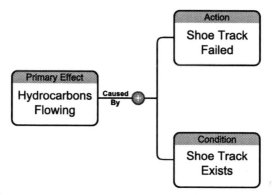

Figure 5.3. First Causal Element for Hydrocarbons Flowing

Looking for Action Causes and Conditional Causes

As the causes present themselves and you place the pieces of the puzzle, do not be concerned with whether they are actions (momentary causes that bring conditions together to cause an effect) or conditions (causes that exist over time prior to an action). Rather, just concentrate on identifying the causal relationships. After you've listed the known causes, go back through the cause-and-effect chart and look for branches. If you have written down an action-type cause, ask yourself what conditions had to be in place for the action to cause the effect. For each conditional cause, make sure you have a corresponding action cause. Remember, we generally find several conditional causes and one action cause in each elemental causal set.

The only value of knowing if a cause is an action or a condition is that it tells us which one is missing and hence which one we need to look for.

When we express a cause or an effect, we see that it has a name and an action. The what of each cause/effect is stated in a noun-verb or verb-noun expression. In the case of a conditional cause, the verb is often understood as "exists" or "is." For an action cause, the verb is the action and the noun is the thing that is acting or being acted upon.

In Figure 5.4, the primary effect is expressed as a modified noun ("Unhappy Customer"). The verb is understood as "exists." The action cause is expressed as a noun ("Computer") and verb ("Failed"). The conditional cause is expressed as a noun ("Customer"). Again, the associated verb is understood to be "exists." When expressing cause-and-effect relationships, we should always attempt to follow these conventions.

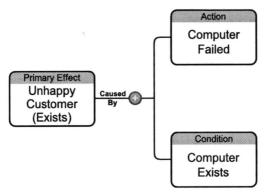

Figure 5.4.   Noun-Verb
Relationships

A valuable part of any incident investigation is the time line of the event. A time line, while usually presented as story elements, gives us a simple understanding of what happened. More importantly, it provides a good starting point for understanding the causal relationships because it often provides a set of action causes. To get an appreciation for the value of a time line, let's take a look at a sequence of events from the Deepwater Horizon Oil Rig Fire and Explosion event that occurred on April 20, 2010.

Time   Time-line Entries

19:55   Negative-pressure test concluded and considered a good test

20:00   Internal blowout preventer and annular preventer opened and pumping of seawater commenced down the drill pipe to displace mud and spacer from the riser

20:52   Calculated that the well went underbalanced and started to flow

21:08   Spacer observed at surface. With pumps off, drill pipe pressure increased from 1,017 psi to 1,263 psi in 5½ minutes. Well inflow calculated at 9 barrels/minute

21:14   Pumps restarted to continue displacement

21:31   Pumps shut down

21:34   Drill pipe pressure increased from 1,210 psi to 1,766 psi

21:38   Hydrocarbons calculated to have passed from well into riser.

21:41   Mud shot up through derrick

21:45   Assistant driller reports that "The well is blowing out . . . and the Toolpusher is shutting it in now."

21:46   Gas hissing noise heard and high-pressure gas discharged from the vents toward the deck

21:47   First gas alarm heard and vibration felt

21:47   Drill pipe pressure started rapidly increasing from 1,200 psi to 5,730 psi

21:48   Main power generation engines started going into overspeed

21:49   Rig lost power; real-time data transmission lost

Estimated first explosion occurred five seconds later

Estimated second explosion occurred ten seconds after first explosion

21:52   Mayday call made from Deepwater Horizon

Every one of these time-line entries is an action cause. By focusing on actions and not on the associated conditional causes, we leave out important causes that might be acted on to provide an effective solution. If we add some effects and conditional causes to this picture, the elemental causal sets begin to emerge. In Figure 5.5, we can start with the action cause of "Hydrocarbons Entered Well" provided by the time line and build on it by adding the effect and a conditional cause. This is only the beginning of documenting many other causes, so at this point stay focused on the action causes as given in the time line and then build on them as you continue to ask why.

In Figure 5.6 another elemental causal set is identified. By evaluating each action cause in the time line, we are able to create some elemental causal sets that will eventually come together to form a complete cause-and-effect chart.

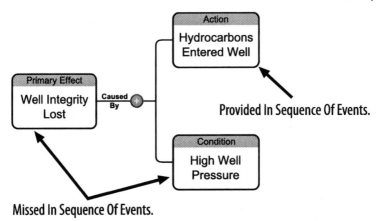

Figure 5.5. Causal Element Developed from
Time-line Action

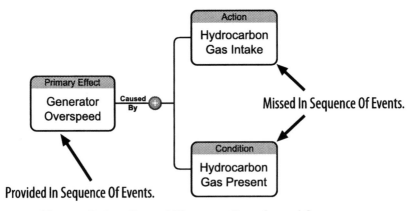

Figure 5.6. Causal Element Developed from
Time-line Action

Each time we develop an elemental causal set, we enrich our understanding of the problem and increase the number of causes, each of which may provide an opportunity to act upon and thus prevent the problem from occurring again.

The best solutions are usually associated with conditional causes, partly because of our greater ability to control conditional causes, whereas people or action causes are less predictable.

Sometimes causes are noncauses. That is, they are nonactions or nonconditions. For example, the action in Figure 5.7 states that the valve was not energized—a nonaction, but listed as an action cause to distinguish it from a conditional cause. The same can occur with conditions. We could have "no firefighters on duty" as a conditional cause.

Sometimes the causal elements create a close-coupled feedback loop like Figure 5.7. In this causal element from the Deepwater Horizon Well incident we see that the solenoid valve could not be energized because of the condition of an electrical fault in the solenoid coil, but that is a conditional cause and we need a corresponding action cause, but there was no action, just a nonaction of "Not Energized." These types of causal sets are difficult for beginners to recognize, but are shown here to help you see different permutations that actions and conditions can take. They are always there, but not always easy to identify because we have never been taught to think causally.

There are two basic types of feedback loops, positive and negative.

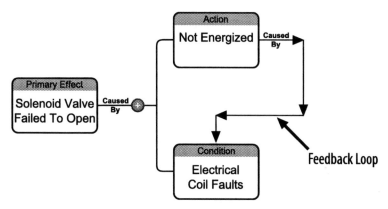

Figure 5.7.   Negative Actions and a
Feedback Loop

Positive feedback in a system is where the increase in a given variable or cause produces a further increase in that variable or cause. The growth in human population is a good example of a positive feedback loop. The more people who exist, the more there are to reproduce and the numbers increase exponentially.

Negative feedback in a system is where the increase in a given variable or cause produces a decrease in another and vise versa. Negative feedback loops often produce destabilizing effects such as war, pestilence, and famine, which often cause a decrease in the human population.

Feedback loops are common in all natural and human systems and add another dimension to the reality of the infinite set. With each feedback loop we add a complexity to reality that is difficult to comprehend or express when using storytelling and categorization.

RealityCharting® provides an easy click of the computer mouse to identify, document, and share feedback loops using a *go-to* reference— something not possible in any other communication formats.

Connect All Causes with the Words "Caused By"

Using "Caused By" helps the mind align causes from the present to the past and thus prevents the tendency to tell stories. Because we are starting with an effect we do not want to recur, we must understand its causes that lie in the past. This process ensures that we follow the fourth element of the cause-and-effect principle, which states that an effect exists only if its causes exist at the same point in time and space. An additional benefit is that it helps avoid storytelling if we follow what I call the "Square One Loop."

> **The Square One Loop** involves following each cause path in a Realitychart until the collective point of ignorance is reached, and then starting over again with the primary effect (square one) and repeating the process.

The Square One Loop holds a key to efficiency and it works like this: As you ask why, immediately input the answer, and ask why again. If you are in a group or team meeting, minimize discussion by inputting the first cause you hear and immediately asking why, thus cutting off further discussion (storytelling) and overanalysis. Continue to ask why until the answers stop coming (called the "point of ignorance") or until things get fuzzy (called the "fuzzy zone"). This is where you can honestly say, "I don't know and neither does anyone else on the team."

Follow each cause path to the point of ignorance, and when you reach your collective point of ignorance, go back to square one (the primary effect) and start asking why again (this represents one loop in the Square One Loop). Try to identify causes between the causes and look for branches (actions and conditions) each time you go through the loop. Repeat the Square One Loop several times or until the ends of every cause path become fuzzy—your point of ignorance. If you want to make assumptions or express opinions, do so within reason. You should be looking for missing causal relationships and making sure you have identified all the causes in each causal element. A good question to ask at this point is "do the causes we currently have always cause the same effect, or are there some other causes needed." This is a test of sufficiency. For example: Every time a car hits another car, does it result in damage? The answer is no, it requires sufficient force to cause damage, so you may need to add a conditional cause that expresses the measure of a cause, be it force, volume, size, or some other measure.

Focusing on "Caused By" as the connecting phrase will minimize unnecessary analysis and storytelling. As you go through the Square One Loop, say, "[The effect] was caused by" with no inflection. Saying "caused by" with a question in your voice elicits a narrow response because it implies one answer. If this does not elicit discussion in your group, ask "why is this cause here," or state the effect and simply ask why. Asking why with no inflection elicits a broader response because it implies no boundaries.

A brief note on the use of the word "ignorance." Like the word "failure," most people get very uncomfortable with these terms because they seem to imply some sort of insult. Understanding our ignorance and our failures is the path to understanding and knowledge, so if these words cause you some angst, turn this around and see them in the positive light they are intended. To do otherwise is a failed strategy—see chapter thirteen for more discussion.

End Each Cause Path with a Question Mark or a Reason for Stopping

Our purpose in asking why is to find our point of ignorance, not to show how smart we are. We need to embrace our ignorance, which should be quite easy now that we understand the notion of the infinite set of causes that is reality. When you get to your point of ignorance, insert a question mark to denote your lack of knowledge and the need to get more information. RealityCharting® allows you to insert a question mark and the text "More Information Needed" with the click of the mouse and the software will automatically put the associated cause into an Action Items Report for further assessment.

Only one in twenty people are capable of admitting they don't know the answer when dealing with a serious question within their expertise. About 95% of the time, when we can't find an answer, we make one up and then spend enormous amounts of time justifying it with various rationalizations. This is a fundamental human reaction that is very detrimental to effective problem solving, so watch for it.

Sometimes a cause path will take us not to our point of ignorance, but to a valid reason for stopping. There are really only four reasons for stopping and RealityCharting® again makes it easy to insert these with the click of a mouse.

Desired Condition—This is the most common reason for stopping and reflects the fact that the event was caused by the pursuit of one or more goals. If you reached your goal or a desired condition, there is no need to continue asking why. If your goal is faulty, that is another matter. Examples of this include "met production goals," "procedure followed," or "service level met."

Lack of Control—This can be an easy excuse for stopping, so make sure the lack of control is outside your or your organization's control before using this reason. Examples are "laws of physics" or "legal requirement."

New Primary Effect—This occurs when you get to a point in the cause path that you need to do a separate analysis. The reasons for a separate analysis can be many, such as outside your control but within another organization's control, or it is within your control but you want to separate it for resource or presentation purposes. This reason is often used as an interim stopping point because you have a separate team working on the details of this cause. When they are done, you can easily import their Realitychart into the final analysis.

Other Cause Paths More Productive—Sometimes you may have solutions that will prevent recurrence and there is no need to go down other cause paths because they are simply not productive or cost too much to pursue. It doesn't make any sense to continue down these cause paths and spend more time and money when you already have effective solutions. This reason for stopping is usually not identified until late in the analysis. This may also be caused by obviously frivolous causes, like the sky is blue.

To learn more about how to construct a Realitychart, watch the following video: http://coach.RealityCharting.com/Book/Node-Menu.

6

Step Three: Provide a Graphical Representation

A picture is worth a thousand words.

—Author unknown

Since the dawn of humanity, we have been using images and diagrams to help us communicate. Because our language does not allow us to effectively communicate the causal relationships of reality, we need another means. Using RealityCharting® software helps produce a more accurate picture of our problems than ever before possible in the history of humankind.

As discussed in chapter one, we are not very good at thinking causally because of the way our brains work and how we communicate. The brain wants to categorize things to make sense of them by relating them to other things we already know and our language and grammar conventions do not allow us to express multiple causes or the infinite set of causes that is reality. Without an easy way to share the known causal relationships of a given event, it is extremely difficult to communicate what we know to other stakeholders.

To overcome this major roadblock to effective solutions and stakeholder buy-in, we need a simple way to graphically represent the causal relationships.

RealityCharting® not only fills this need, it provides an intuitive structured process. As the name *RealityCharting* implies, this powerful tool creates a cause-and-effect chart of your reality or, more importantly, a chart of the common reality from the perspective of all stakeholders.

For a complete overview of the software watch the following video at http://coach.RealityCharting.com/Book/Overview.

RealityCharting has over thirty concise Help videos that show you how every feature works. It also has a Wizard to guide you through the process. To view these videos, go to http://Help.RealityCharting.com/features.

Structure of Causal Relationships

As we learned in the last chapter, expressing causal relationships requires a primary effect and at least two causes in the form of at least one action and one or more conditions. We also learned that to avoid storytelling and make sure we go from the present to the past, we connect the causes with the words "Caused By." And to ensure that we don't stop too soon we need to end each cause path with a reason for stopping or admit our ignorance and identify that more information is needed. A good graphical representation also needs to identify how we know that the causes we provided are legitimate, so we also need to list the evidence for each cause. We will discuss evidence in more detail in the next chapter, but Figure 6.1 provides a simple example of a Realitychart that includes all of these elements.

This is a very simple example to show the basic elements of a principle-based cause-and-effect chart. As we continue to ask why of each known cause we can see how complex reality can become. The more complicated the event, the more complex the cause-and-effect chart becomes.

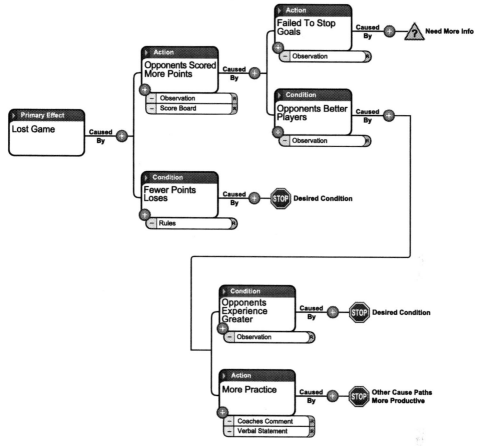

Figure 6.1. Lost Game Realitychart

Getting back to the Deepwater Horizon event, we can see from the following example in Figure 6.2 how complicated causal relationships can become and hence why it is impossible to communicate this complexity any other way. Figure 6.2 is only part of a chart with thirty-nine causes and it only addresses one of the eight key findings and many causes are missing because the report is so limited.

Philosophies—

Charting is not an exact science, so there is no single correct cause-and-effect chart for a given event. We are not trying to find the truth or the mythical root cause. We are trying to identify effective solutions. The cause-and-effect chart is simply a representation of the common reality of those who create it. If you find yourself disagreeing or arguing over the "right" causes, you have missed the point of RealityCharting. The chart will

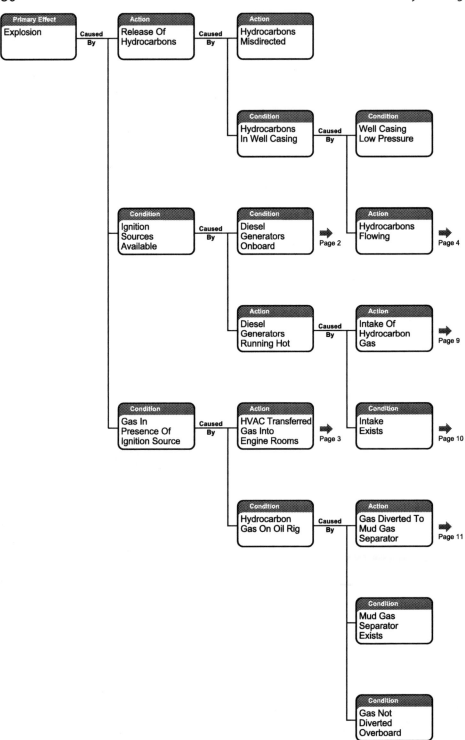

Figure 6.2. Deepwater Horizon Explosion

provide a starting point from which to find effective solutions, and while it is not possible to make it perfect, it will be much better than any other problem-solving method you might use.

We are often hindered by our willingness to surrender our individuality in a group or team setting, so go outside your group to find different perspectives and thus additional causes.

Also beware of parochial thinking—it often causes a narrow point of view and we stop too soon in our quest for causes. Try to find other knowledgeable people to review your chart before you finish it. Listen to them with an open mind and if you can't explain the chart, you probably don't understand the causes.

Learn to be humble and help others do the same. Be authentic and honest with others.

Effective Chart-Building Strategies—

Look for actions and conditions, but if you don't see them, do not get bogged down. It is more important to keep moving through the Square One Loop than anything else. If you stop asking why or get bogged down, people lose interest and the process comes to a halt. Follow each cause path to your point of ignorance or make a conscious decision to stop asking why. Do not discuss solutions until you are finished with the Realitychart.

When team members cannot agree, or to get the team started, the facilitator can prepare a strawman Realitychart. It is always easier to criticize than to create. (A strawman is an argument set up for discussion so as to be easily refuted, like a trial balloon.)

If you ask why and no answers come, look for answers in people, procedures, and hardware. It also helps to look for differences; and when you find them, start asking why. With this strategy, you will find yourself back in the cause-and-effect mode. During one investigation, I found myself at the end of a cause chain because when I asked the welder if he had done anything differently during the incident that led to the problem, he said he could not think of anything, yet something had changed to cause the problem of the weld not being correct. As I continued to ask questions, I found the preheating procedure was not performed properly. Once I found this difference, I could begin to ask why again. When something has been working for a period of time and a problem occurs, it is best to start by looking for differences or changes in the procedures or process.

Often, it is beneficial to start the chart by listing all possible causes. Because the causes may not have evidence at this time, the connecting logic may be "or" rather than "and." For example, the primary effect is caused by cause "A" *or* cause "B" *or* cause "C", and so on. As you establish evidence for two or more parallel causes, the "or" logic disappears and the final logic becomes "and" (that is, the primary effect is caused by "Cause A" and "B" and "C". If you choose to show possibilities on the final chart, they must be labeled accordingly, because all parallel cause boxes are understood to be related by "and" logic. "Or" logic means you don't know. It is caused by this "or" that. By adding evidence that the causes exist, the "or" must be changed to "and." RealityCharting® provides a simple drop-down menu that allows you to identify any causal relationship with "or" logic as shown in the Node Menu video mentioned at the end of chapter five.

Additional Aids to Communication—

In large organizations stakeholders commonly know their roles in the work process, yet in most cases, no one knows the entire process. As a result, when we begin to solve a problem within our work process, we fail to communicate because our belief in common sense dictates that everyone knows what's going on. To overcome this problem, it is best to start the problem-solving process by creating a flow chart of the work process in question. Every player must be involved in creating the flow chart. A supervisor may create a strawman chart to get started, but every player should review and comment on the legitimacy of the flow chart. As the process diagram or flow chart is developed, errors, omissions, and misunderstandings will surface; and you can begin asking why and create a Realitychart. You may also have to create or find pictures, diagrams, or drawings of equipment to help in understanding the causes.

Solving Problems Effectively Using RealityCharting®

Using RealityCharting® software will produce a more accurate picture of your problems than ever before possible. For groups it creates a common reality and a visual map that facilitates dialog through appreciative understanding. By appreciatively understanding all perspectives, we understand important causal relationships that would not otherwise be found. Without the Realitychart, we are left to linear thinking and storytelling. Therefore, we need to appreciatively understand all perspectives and use RealityCharting® to the best of our ability.

This is not always easy without some practice because appreciative understanding and RealityCharting are a new way of thinking for most people. However, as Oliver Wendell Holmes said, "Man's mind, once stretched by a new idea, never regains its original dimensions." To overcome the anxiety associated with implementing this new way of thinking, RealityCharting® software will not only provide a step-by-step map, it will ensure an accurate chart every time. Those who have used RealityCharting for some time, report back that it has fundamentally changed their lives by improving their day-to-day problem-solving skills because they are now thinking causally rather than storytelling or categorizing.

RealityCharting® comes with a Learning Center where anyone can learn the RealityCharting process and the software at the same time. To learn more, go to http://coach.realitycharting.com.

The more we use these tools, the more natural they become and the long-term payback is a more accurate way of thinking because we realize things don't just happen. We see that every effect has causes, and most of them can be known and easily documented using RealityCharting®. The common reality resulting from this process allows effective communication between all stakeholders. If any stakeholder wants to add to the reality at any time, they only have to put their causes and evidence on the chart. If it leads to a better solution, then it has value and will be accepted by everyone. No arguments and no confrontations.

Because problem solving is about effective solutions, the ability to get all stakeholders to buy into the solutions makes the RealityCharting process unique in the world of problem solving.

7

Step Four: Provide Evidence

Don't leave inferences to be drawn when evidence can be presented.

—Richard Wright

Evidence is defined as data that supports our conclusions, but to be effective it must be void of opinion and emotions. It provides value to the problem-solving process when it is associated with a specific cause and of the highest quality. Starting at the highest quality, evidence types are sensed, inferred, intuited, and emotional. Each one is discussed in detail in this chapter.

This is perhaps the most important step in the process because it helps us ensure that we are not fooling ourselves or misrepresenting the situation with opinions or putting a political spin on reality.

Over the years, I have had an occasion or two to help local governments solve their problems using the RealityCharting process. The politicians were initially excited about this help, but they soon learned that you have to have evidence to support the causal relationships and this often made it hard for them to meet their political objectives. Politicians by their very nature are good storytellers and use stories and the gift to gab to persuade others. Since, as we learned earlier, stories are linear and use inference and innuendo to communicate causes and are often void of evidence, the politicians soon abandoned causal thinking to make their points or solve the problems before them. And because the masses are not capable of thinking causally either, we stumble down the path of ignorance together and then wonder why we fail to meet our goals.

Evidence Defined

But what is evidence, or how do we know we have good evidence?" We seem to have an innate understanding of what evidence is, and I find very few people have difficulty establishing causal evidence where it is available. However, when asked to define evidence or explain what makes good evidence, most people can't do it.

The dictionary defines evidence as data that supports a conclusion. We conclude something exists either by directly sensing it with one of our five senses or by inference through causal relationships. We also use intuition and feeling as the basis of conclusions, which are more subtle forms of inference. Let's examine the different types of evidence.

Sensed evidence is the highest quality of evidence and consists of knowing by way of sight, sound, smell, touch, or taste. In the example in Figure 7.1, all evidence is sensory—it was seen or heard. Evidence is best stated by telling which sense was used. If something was observed, we know through our eyes; if we smelled smoke, then we know through our nose.

Inferred evidence is known by repeatable causal relationships. Evidence that someone is happy can be known by a smile on their face. That is, we

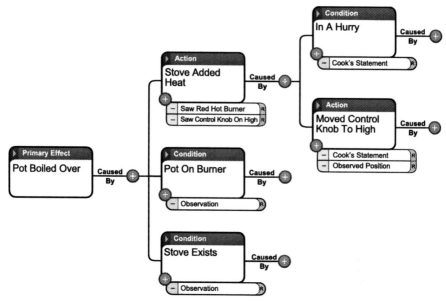

Figure 7.1. Sensed Evidence

infer happiness by knowing the following repeatable causal relationship: "Smile" *caused by* "Facial Muscles Moving" *caused by* "Happiness."

The best evidence is direct observation using one or more of our senses. For example, I know fire because I see flames, feel heat, and hear crackling. Inferred evidence is less desirable but may be all we have. Using this same example, we may know fire by seeing smoke, smelling smoke, and tasting smoke, but this is an inferred causal relationship that assumes fire causes smoke.

Causes and evidence are often interchangeable because of the way we use inferred evidence. I may legitimately state that smoke is evidence of fire. But it is also correct to say smoke is caused by fire, and the evidence of the fire is my observation of smoke. If I can't see the flames of the fire, using smoke as inferred evidence may be acceptable, but it is a lower quality of evidence. The perceived smoke may actually be mist, dust, or fog and there is no fire.

Because inferred causal relationships are not always well understood, they are not necessarily as reliable as sensed evidence. For example, if I believe that wind is caused by clouds, as I did as a child, then it is logically inferred that big clouds are evidence of high winds. If this causal relationship helps me understand my world and is repeatable within that world, then I will continue to infer that big clouds are evidence of high winds, even though it is scientifically false. We can only know what we know.

If inferred evidence is all we have, we should use it. Sometimes the only way to know something is by inference. For example, humans cannot directly sense the pressure in a tank. We may sense pressure if we let it out and it impinges on our skin; but while it is in the tank, we can only know the pressure indirectly through inferred causal relationships. Reading a pressure gauge may be evidence of high pressure. We know the mechanics and the physics that cause the pressure gauge to work, so the pressure is known through a repeatable causal relationship of the instrument. The pressure indicator reading is caused by a lever moving, which is caused by a bellows expanding, which is caused by high pressure. Because this causal path is known and repeatable, we do not need to write it out. "Pressure Indicator Reading" is adequate evidence of high pressure if everyone who reads the Realitychart knows this relationship is valid and repeatable. If it is not understood by everyone or is not repeatable, the cause path should be explored to verify that the causes exist with sensed evidence.

Because inferred evidence relies on the assumption that the reader knows the causal relationship, it should be readily verifiable. If it is not, the causal relationship should be included in the Realitychart. For example, consider the inferred evidence in Figure 7.2.

"Fuel Vaporized" is evidenced by the temperature of 285 °F, and this can be readily verified by looking at a fuel vaporization chart so that is also provided as evidence. The fuel vaporization chart is empirical data resulting from observing and recording known causal relationships and as such it is inferred evidence. "High Tank Temperature" is evidenced by reading the

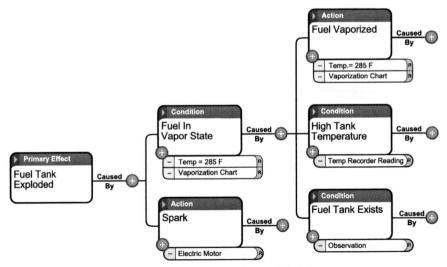

Figure 7.2.   Inferred Evidence

temperature recorder. The reading of the recorder is sensory evidence of inferred evidence. The instrumentation that causes the recorder to work is known by repeatable causal relationships. But what about "Spark" being evidenced by "Electric Motor"? The inference is that because electric motors can make sparks, the electric motor is evidence of a spark. But this is not necessarily so because not all motors make sparks. If we knew it, it would be better to indicate evidence of a spark as "Burn Mark" or "Saw Electric Arc" and show the spark as caused by "Electric Motor." The point is that when using inferred evidence, be very careful that you know the causal relationships being expressed with the inference. Furthermore, if the inference is derived from some device or instrument such as a temperature recorder, it may be necessary to validate the calibration of the instrument to assure that the evidence is indeed correct.

Intuition is inferred evidence based on both reason and emotions but, because it occurs at a subconscious level, we are not capable of explaining where it comes from. Consequently, using intuition as evidence presents a risk. An example of intuited evidence is shown in Figure 7.3. It is understandable that "Inadequate Marketing" could be evidenced by "Manager's Opinion," and that "Fewer Sales Hours Worked" could be evidenced by "Intuition," but this is certainly not very high quality evidence. We may choose to accept this as evidence, but we should be suspect of the potential risks of acting on these causes until we know more causal relationships with better evidence.

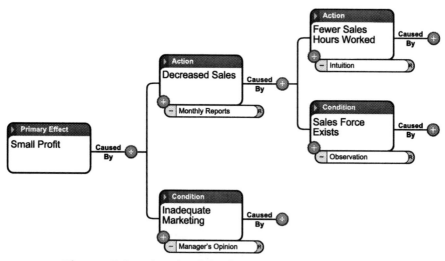

Figure 7.3. Intuited Evidence

Emotional evidence is shown in Figure 7.4 where "Sensed Danger" is evidenced by feeling scared. We see that emotional evidence is inferred evidence from a known repeatable causal relationship, but the five senses are not involved in the knowing process. Emotions and feelings exist in the limbic system within the old reptilian portion of the brain, while the senses are located in the cortex along with reasoning. As such, emotions and reasoning are not well connected. Emotions are very real and they should not be ignored as evidence of a cause, but they should be held suspect because they are not always reliable.

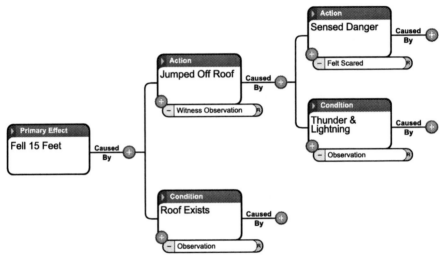

Figure 7.4.   Emotional Evidence

While most people seem to intuitively understand what constitutes evidence and what does not, the difference is not universally known. Sometimes certain words get in our way. The most misused word I've encountered is "fact." For most people a fact is something that is absolutely known to exist in their world and yours. The problem with this notion is that it ignores perception, as discussed in chapter one. What may be a "fact" to you may inspire a great debate in your neighbor. To avoid this issue, I suggest you never use this word or redefine it to include evidence.

> **Fact:** A cause supported by evidence.

Facts have no value unless used in the realm of causal relationships. It is a fact that the sign is red because we can see it, but this statement has absolutely no value whatsoever until such time as it is placed into a causal relationship. The red sign caused me to stop or "Stopped Moving Caused by Red Sign." Therefore, meaningful facts are always evidence-based causes in a set of other causes.

Sometimes we find contradictory causes and evidence. Contradictory causes should be documented on the Realitychart and evidence should then be sought to explain the contradiction or establish one cause as more likely than the other by virtue of preponderance (such as weight, quantity, or importance). The Realitychart works well to show contradictions because it lays out all perspectives. Every stakeholder can see the relationships between other causes and supporting evidence. If one cause has a preponderance of evidence and a competing cause has poor evidence, the chart allows both to be represented and both causes can be discussed according to the quality of their evidence. If a solution is attached to a cause chain with poorly evidenced causes, then it clearly shows the risk being taken. If the solution is attached to a cause chain with well-evidenced causes, the effectiveness will be assured.

Often, the problem with evidence is not being able to find it. If you cannot find evidence RealityCharting® automatically inserts a question mark in the evidence box and adds it to an Actions Item Report for further evaluation.

To see how RealityCharting® helps you add evidence watch the video at http://coach.RealityCharting.com/Book/Evidence.

8

Step Five: Determine if Causes Are Sufficient and Necessary

How many legs does a dog have if you call the tail a leg? Four.
Calling a tail a leg doesn't make it a leg.

—Abraham Lincoln

Ensuring that the causes of each effect are necessary and sufficient is like putting icing on a cake. Without it, the product of your labor is incomplete. The fourth principle of causation helps us identify the necessary causes by making sure all the causes of an effect occur at the same place in space and in the same time frame. To help determine if the causes are sufficient, we should ask: "Does this effect always occur when the stated causes come together at the same point in space and time?" and "Are these causes sufficient to cause the effect, or are there other causes?"

Causal analysis is a difficult process even for experienced investigators. Even after understanding the basic causal structure of reality and the ease of using RealityCharting®, finding the action and condition causes can be problematic. Because we have never had to think this way and because the brain wants to make things simpler than they are, we naturally filter out many causes. In his legendary book, *The Fifth Discipline*, Peter Senge states that "cause and effect are not closely related in time and space." He goes on to explain that most people think the cause to which we attach our solution is only a cause or two away from the symptom or effect we wish to change.[1] In other words, we tend to try and make reality much simpler than it really is and in doing so implement very poor solutions. Only by fully understanding all the causal relationships of a given event are we assured of effective solutions.

Necessary Causes

To help overcome this human condition I find that it helps to carefully examine each causal set and make sure that the causes actually occur at the same point in time and space *and* to make the time frame being observed as short as possible. Try to create a video in your mind's eye of the event and use your "stop-action" button to look carefully at causes at a given point in time. Let's take a look at an example of this. In Figure 8.1 we see that the "Broken Leg" was caused by two causes, "Jumped Off Roof" and "Fell 15 Feet." While these are causes of the broken leg, are they really occurring at the same point in time and space?

Let's look a little closer. Run the video in your mind's eye and see the bone actually breaking and ask what the causes are at this point in the video. Is it really "Jumped Off Roof? Jumping off the roof was farther

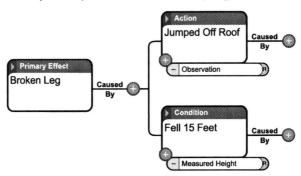

Figure 8.1.   First Look

back in time wasn't it? So, looking more closely, we see that it is excess force on the bone, so perhaps we should expand on this as we did in Figure 8.2, where we show the cause of the broken leg to be excess force and impacting the ground, and falling fifteen feet. Certainly makes more sense doesn't it? Furthermore, we see that "Falling 15 Feet" is actually caused by the act of jumping off the roof, not a companion cause as shown in Figure 8.1.

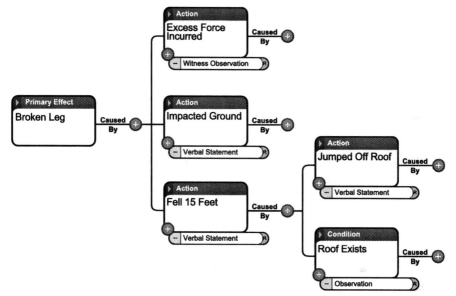

Figure 8.2. Second Look

But wait a minute, if we look closely at Figure 8.2 we see a violation of the principle that there should be one action cause and one or more conditional causes for "Broken Leg." Figure 8.2 shows three actions at the same point in time and space. While it is possible to have three actions at the same point in time and space, and these are certainly causes of the broken leg, are they actually occurring at the same point in time and space and what is the conditional cause? Let's turn on our video again and see if Figure 8.3 shows a better picture.

As you can see now, we have a much better perspective of the causes in space and time and see that there are actually three causal sets between "Broken Leg" and "Jumped Off Roof." Of note, we could add even more causes to "Excess Force Incurred," such as the weight of the person who fell, but I left these and other causes off to preserve space and still make the point. As we will discuss more fully in the next chapter on solutions, having more causes provides more opportunities to affect

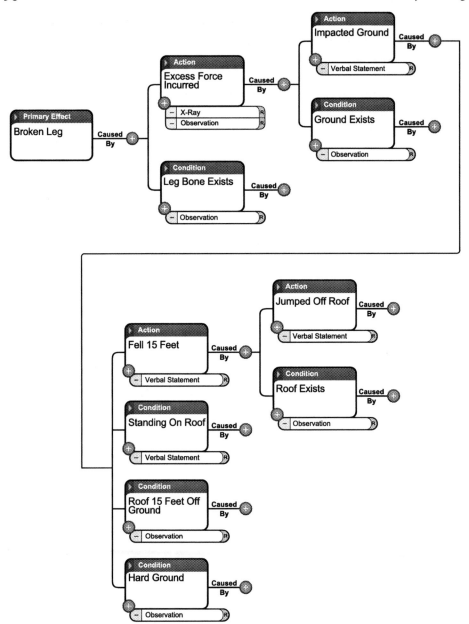

Figure 8.3. Third Look

the outcome of the event. For example, we could make the ground softer or ask why is the person standing on the roof in the first place and maybe eliminate the need. When we only list the two original causes of "Jumped Off Roof" and "Fell 15 Feet," there are too few causes to attach effective solutions to.

By carefully making sure you adhere to the fourth principle of cause and effect, you will identify the necessary causes of each effect on your chart.

Sufficiency

In addition to making sure that each causal set has causes that occur at the same point in space and time, you should be looking for sufficiency. To do this, you should always ask if there are other causes that could mitigate or exacerbate the effect. This often helps identify unseen causes. For example, if "Car Wrecked" is caused by "Car Struck" and "Car Existed," you may find more causes by looking for exacerbating causes. For example, we should ask "Are these causes sufficient to cause the car to be wrecked, or are there other causes?" In answering this question of sufficiency, we see that for the car to be wrecked, there also had to be sufficient force. Another way to ask the question of sufficiency is to ask "Does this effect always occur when the stated causes come together at the same point in space and time?" If the answer is no, then you are probably missing some causes; find them and add them to the chart. Each time you add a new cause, the cause-and-effect principle dictates that it can create at least two more causes unless you choose to stop asking why. For example: If you add "Sufficient Force" as another cause of "Car Wrecked," then it begs further why questions, such as "Traveling Too Fast?", "Distracted?", "Brakes Failed?" etc.

To help with the need to identify necessary and sufficient causes, RealityCharting® asks the following questions of each causal element using the advanced logic check feature.

1. Do the causes of this effect exist at the same time?
2. Do the causes of this effect exist in the same place?

If the answer to each question is yes, then the causal relationship meets the fourth principle.

RealityCharting® also performs a causal logic check to determine if the causes are sufficient to cause the effect. It does this by asking the following question of each cause in a causal element.

If you remove this cause, will the effect still exist?

If the answer to this question is no, then the cause is necessary for the causal relationship and should stay on the chart. If the answer is yes, it should be removed or repositioned.

To see how these rule checks work in RealityCharting® go to http://coach.RealityCharting.com/Book/Advanced-Rules.

Correlations Are Not Causes

Almost every day we hear some new report or read some news article about some scary comparison, like "Another indicator of global warming is that in the past 100 years, damage from hurricanes has steadily and significantly increased." These simpleminded arguments come from seemingly intelligent people, but they have no causal basis. In 1949, Dr. Benjamin Sandler released a book in North Carolina that stated polio was caused by consuming ice cream and soda. The basis for his claim was a direct correlation between the consumption of these products and the incidence of new polio cases. He went on to describe some bizarre causal connections between the ice cream and the nervous system, which again had no evidenced based causes, only more correlations.

Correlations do not constitute a causal relationship, only evidence-based causal relationships do. The reason damage from hurricanes has increased over the past 100 years is that more people live near the water, caused by an ever-increasing standard of living which allows us to spend more money on homes, levies, and canals, which further exacerbate flooding by preventing the natural flow of water into the river deltas and wetlands. While it is possible that global warming could cause more hurricanes, there is no causal evidence to support this notion. To close-couple the effect of "Increased Damages" as being caused by "Global Warming" is an example of what Peter Senge observed, that most people's thinking is fundamentally flawed when it comes to cause-and-effect relationships.

As for ice cream causing polio, luckily this idea didn't go too far and we developed the polio vaccine using cause-based science instead. Polio is caused by poliovirus not ice cream or soda or calcium or any of the other pseudoscience nonsense perpetuated by the media and Internet quacks who thrive on ignorant people. Remember, the news media is a multibillion dollar business and, like all business, their primary purpose is to stay in business. They do this by selling stories and the better the stories, the more sales they make. One way to sell more stories is to scare us and using correlations instead of evidence-based causal relationships facilitates this. Furthermore, as we learned in chapter one, storytelling cannot effectively convey the causal relationships that are reality and this is exacerbated when those writing the stories use correlations to convey the message.

Baloney Detection Kit

In 1997, Carl Sagan wrote about ways to separate "fact" from fiction or, more specifically, science from pseudoscience in his book, *The Demon Haunted World: Science as a Candle in the Dark*.[2] The following is based on that work and correlates it to what we have learned so far in this book.

1. **Seek independent facts.** Remember, a fact is a cause supported by sensed evidence and should be independently verified by you before it can be deemed legitimate. If you cannot find sensed evidence of causal relationships you should be skeptical.

2. **Welcome open debate on all points of view.** Suspend judgment about the event or claim until all cause paths have been pursued to your satisfaction using RealityCharting®.

3. **Always challenge authority.** Ask to be educated. Ask the expert how they came to know what they know. If they cannot explain it to your satisfaction using evidence-based causal relationships then be very skeptical.

4. **Consider more than one hypothesis.** The difference between a genius and a normal person is that when asked to solve a problem the genius doesn't look for the right answer, he or she looks for how many possible solutions he or she can find. A genius fundamentally understands that there is always another possibility, limited by our fundamental ignorance of what is really happening.

5. **Don't defend a position because it is yours.** All ideas are prototypical because there is no way we can really know all the causes. Seek to understand before seeking to be understood.

6. **Try to quantify what you think you know.** Can you put numbers to it?

7. **If there is a chain of causes presented, every link must work.** Use RealityCharting® to verify that the chain of causes meets the advanced logic checks defined above and that the causes are sufficient in and of themselves.

8. **Use Occam's razor to decide between two hypothesis**; If two explanations appear to be equally viable, choose the simpler one if you must. Nature loves simplicity.

9. **Try to prove your hypothesis wrong.** Every truth is prototypical and the purpose of science is to disprove that which we think we know.

10. **Use carefully designed experiments to test all hypotheses.**

For a different slant on the Baloney Detection Kit, go to www.skeptic. com.

References

1. Peter Senge. *The Fifth Discipline*. New York: Currency Doubleday (1990).
2. Carl Sagan. *The Demon Haunted World: Science as a Candle in the Dark*. New York: Ballantine Books.

9

Step Six: Identify Effective Solutions

> For every complex problem there is a solution that is simple, neat, and wrong.
>
> —H. L. Mencken

Identifying effective solutions is the primary purpose of problem solving and there are some subtleties we need to understand. Solutions act on one or more causes in the cause-and-effect chain without regard for position. So the notion of a "root" cause or a magic bullet at the end of a chain becomes meaningless. If we must retain the notion of "root causes," then they are the ones to which we attach solutions. And, since any given problem has an infinite number of causes, there are an infinite number of possible solutions.

What we need to find are the best solutions. As we will see in this chapter, these solutions must meet the following criteria:

1. *Prevent recurrence.*
2. *Be within your control.*
3. *Meet your goals and objectives.*
4. *Not Cause other problems that you are aware of.*

We have been led to believe that effective problem solving can be had by finding the root cause at the end of a chain of causes. On the surface, this seems to make sense; but on examination it is overly simplistic because it ignores the infinite set of causes.

Our world is not linear and therefore this logic is overly simplistic and grossly ineffective. As we have seen, our world is made up of an infinite set of causes all connected through causal relationships. Some of these relationships are complicated by feedback loops. Some causes seem to come out of nowhere (the subconscious mind) but all should lead to a point of ignorance. The beginning and end of causation are determined by our knowledge and understanding of the problem.

Once we understand the nonlinearity of our universe, limiting oneself to a linear understanding such as the Five Whys method makes for terribly ineffective solutions. By understanding that there are an infinite number of causes connected in many ways, we begin to see that an infinite number of possible solutions exist. We may only need to affect one cause in a chain so that the problem does not occur—or we may need to attack several causes.

These causes do not have to be at the end of a chain as the notion of root cause would have us believe. Indeed, the best solution may be to remove the very first cause, or as we have learned to call it, the primary effect. For example, for some people the best solution to human error would be to eliminate all employees. If this is possible and allows us to meet our goals and objectives, then it may be the best solution. But we can't know that until we understand the causal relationships that govern the situation or system. The system may require human interaction, in which case removing all humans would not meet our goals and objectives.

Solution Defined

From this discussion, we can see that a solution can be defined as follows:

> **Solution:** An action taken upon a cause to affect a desired condition.

Generally, the action is to remove, change, or otherwise control a cause. Sometimes the action is to not act, such as not smoking to prevent cancer. However, this is merely semantics because the cancer is caused by smoking and the solution is to remove "smoking"; thus, we are acting on a cause.

The desired condition or outcome becomes the focal point of any solution. The purpose of problem solving is to establish conditional causes in the form of a solution or solutions that allow us to accomplish our goals and objectives—to move from the undesired condition to the desired condition.

For problems that have already occurred, a primary goal is to prevent recurrence. For problems that may happen in the future, the goal is to prevent occurrence. If our goals and objectives are to produce something safely and efficiently, then we need to know those goals and objectives before we set up the conditions that will allow safe and efficient production to occur. We must establish conditions such that when human actions occur, they will cause a safe condition and an efficient process or system. No system involving humans is perfect. As unacceptable effects occur in the process, we can go back and understand the problem causes and change them to accomplish our goals. In complicated systems where humans are involved, the number of variables is enormous so we are continually solving problems. This process varies significantly from problem to problem and group to group depending on the personalities and experience, so there is no right way to find solutions, but they must be based on understanding the causal relationships.

To understand the solutions phase of the problem-solving process in more detail, let's examine one way to find solutions and then explore some guidelines for dealing with outliers.

Standard Solution-Finding Process

To find solutions for negative problems that we want to prevent from recurring, the best solutions must:

> Prevent recurrence.
> Be within our control.
> Meet our goals and objectives.
> Not cause other problems.

The basic process is as follows:

- *Start on the right side of the Realitychart and begin challenging the causes. We challenge the causes by asking why is this cause here? What could we do to remove, change, or control it such that the primary effect does not occur? Offer possible solutions for each cause and write them down. RealityCharting® provides an easy way to do this. When challenging the causes, there are no rules but there are guidelines that will make this step easier and more effective. Working top to bottom and then right to left is one of those guidelines. When finished with the upper right cause, move down to the cause below it in the same vertical position. When you get to the bottom of that column, go back to the top and move left one space, offering solutions for each cause along the way. The RealityCharting® Wizard Step 3, Identify Solutions, does this automatically for you. If you want to address a specific cause on the chart, which often happens late in the investigation, a Solution Tool is provided that allows you to select any given cause and attach solutions to it at any time.*

- *Make no judgments about possible solutions at this time. Move as quickly as possible from top to bottom and right to left. Do not waste time trying to analyze every solution at this time. Staying lighthearted at this stage is very helpful. Don't overthink or judge at this time.*

- *Work your way left to the primary effect challenging causes as you go. Be careful to look at every cause or elemental causal set. If nothing comes to mind, move on. Don't dwell on your inability to offer a solution for every cause. Sometimes a short linear causal set within the chart becomes the target for optimum solutions because the other cause chains are clearly outside your control or so incomplete as to require a major research effort to find all the causes. If this is the case, focus on that causal chain and scrutinize it thoroughly. The solutions phase often results in adding more causes to the chart because you realize you stopped too soon or missed some branches. Take the time to add these new insights.*

- *Be open to creative ideas. More on this later.*

- *After you have exhausted your creative juices and challenged each cause, check your solutions against the solution criteria. Again, RealityCharting® provides an easy way to do this. Once you have identified which solutions meet the criteria you can select which ones you want to implement and they are automatically placed in a report.*

Now, let's examine in more detail the process of identifying the best solutions.

Solution Criteria

Everyone has their own opinion and favorite solution, so what makes one solution better than the next one? Or a better question is what makes one solution more effective than the next one?

No matter what the event-based problem is, the solutions must have certain characteristics for them to work, and "work" is the operative word here. For many years I ran an experiment where I asked people to evaluate a problem and identify what they think is the best solution. Most people have been taught the silly notion that there is one right answer. And, of course, the right answer is usually their answer. They argue with one another and use various forms of persuasion to get their solutions accepted by the group. They fail to recognize that there is no such thing as a right or wrong answer to event-based problems. When asked what characterizes an effective solution, "the solution must work" is the most common answer. But what does "must work" mean?

After analyzing over 25,000 answers to this question, I found the answers will always fit into what we can call solution criteria. The best solutions must meet the following criteria:

1. Prevent recurrence, to include similar occurrences at different locations.
2. Be within your control.
3. Meet your goals and objectives.
4. Not cause other unacceptable problems, to include not costing too much.

Assuming we are dealing with a problem that has already occurred, preventing recurrence is essential. Preventing recurrence means that it does not happen again for the same (known) set of causes. Anything other than this is a failure to understand the problem. While this is not always possible because we may fail to see all the causes, we should strive for a 100% nonrepeat.

Solutions must be within our control or they will not work. It is a common human tendency to identify solutions that require other people to act. If you are using the RealityCharting process correctly, this will not happen because all stakeholders will be involved and everyone will take responsibility for the solutions within their control.

Sometimes a solution does not appear to be within your control because it requires higher-level approval. If your cause-and-effect chart has been prepared properly, you will be more likely to convince those who have the authority of the value and efficacy of the solution. The Realitychart can significantly expand your sphere of influence because it is not just another opinion-laced story. It is evidence-based causal relationships, which are hard to ignore, and if the reviewer does find issues with your chart, engage them and include their perspective.

The criteria that causes such a wide variety of possible solutions is the need for solutions to meet our goals and objectives. Most businesses exist to make money, so the solutions should provide a maximum return on investment (ROI). Many companies have an established ROI requirement before implementing a solution. An alternative to measuring ROI is to measure and correct the number of problems above some threshold criteria, for instance, all events costing more than $50,000 in lost revenue. If over time the number of events exceeding this level of concern goes to zero, then your problem-solving process has been effective. If your company is interested in continuous improvement, the threshold criteria should be evaluated and changed according to your goals and objectives.

An important aspect of the solution criteria is the "you" or "your." Your control and your goals mean the solution is owned by those who are going to be responsible for the failure—no one else. The implications of this are multifaceted. It means that no outside organizations have the right to second-guess the solutions unless they are willing to accept the consequences of failure. It also means all stakeholders must understand what their goals and objectives are before they can be expected to be effective problem solvers. Many employees simply have no idea what their goals and objectives are, so they have been set up to fail as effective problem solvers.

Every solution is directly related to the purpose for solving the problem. When employees interject their own purposes into the solution, they may or may not coincide with the purpose of the team or organization. Look for these biases when evaluating solutions. For example, if the purpose of an organization is to operate safely, the solution to a production problem cannot include creating a safety hazard. Unfortunately, we humans find it difficult to recognize all our goals and objectives when considering problem solutions. We tend to be myopic and only recognize one goal or purpose for a given problem. While many organizations today have a set of company goals in the form of mission statements and strategies, these are rarely internalized by every employee.

Each member of an organization understands their role differently. In large organizations employees often see themselves as part of a group. Engineers may form their own understanding of what their contributions to the company goals are, and it is different from the other groups. Operators, maintenance people, and sales people all see their contributions differently. They form a group identity that sets them apart from other groups. When it comes time to work together to solve company problems, people may be divided into different camps looking out for the interests of their group. If you find this thinking, it is essential that you write down the goals and objectives associated with the problem at hand. One obvious goal is to prevent recurrence, but other goals may be to make a 20% ROI or to have zero customer complaints. Each company goal needs to be defined in more detail relative to the problem you are working on.

Because purpose and solutions are so closely related, finding the best solutions often becomes an iterative process of discovery. The causal relationships often begin to fill out with more causes between the causes as potential solutions are discovered. RealityCharting® easily accommodates changes at this stage.

Multiple Solutions

If you followed all the rules in constructing your Realitychart, preventing recurrence may be assured regardless of which solution(s) you chose. However, in some cases 100% assurance is not guaranteed because your ability to control the cause may be limited, such as only being able to slow a leak rather than eliminate it. In these cases one solution may prevent recurrence 90% of the time, while another solution will prevent recurrence another 9% of the time, thus giving you an assurance of 99% prevention. If this meets your goals and objectives, that may be where you stop. Only you can set these standards of quality and excellence. Depending on the significance and consequence of failure, you may be happy with 85% assurance of a nonrepeat.

Solution Guidelines

In the course of identifying solutions, often some solutions do not meet all the criteria but still provide value. We may choose to implement them and this is acceptable, but make sure to identify which cause it attacks. Also, identify these solutions for what they are. If they are not required to prevent recurrence, but will improve the situation, then make this clear. Sometimes we include pet solutions into an inappropriate problem, which results in spending money on something that does not prevent recurrence.

It is not unusual to discover a very good solution that does not seem to be connected to any of the causes on the chart. The solution seems to come out of nowhere. (*Nowhere* is defined as the subconscious mind that is always at work on our problems.) When this occurs, it helps to ask what causes does the solution attack and follow this line of questions to discover a whole new set of causes. Usually we are able to connect the solution with causes on our existing Realitychart, but it may take some exploring. We often know things in a visceral sense, called "gut feel" or intuition. This understanding of the world is held in the part of the brain known as "the emotional center" or limbic system. It is not well connected to the cerebral cortex and the language center, so we don't have a direct command of it, but it is there nonetheless.[1] Do not ignore these feelings because they may hold important insights to effective solutions. Try to document them on the Realitychart.

Solutions should always be specific actions. It makes no sense to attack a specific problem with nonspecific solutions. If the problem was "no money," the solution shouldn't be "get some." Do not include solutions such as review, analyze, or investigate. Such solutions are a copout as they are really saying we don't know what the problem is and won't know until we can gather more causes and evidence. Avoid this denial and state that you don't know what the causes are. Implement mitigating solutions until you can investigate further.

If an ancillary solution is to further investigate or review and the main solutions will prevent recurrence, then this is acceptable, but list these ancillary solutions on a separate tracking list. This will avoid the auditors' complaint that you have not completed this commitment.

Avoid solutions that include the prefix of "re" such as retrain. Avoid the favorite solutions such as the following:

- *punish*
- *reprimand*
- *replace the broken part*
- *investigate*
- *revise the procedure*
- *write a new procedure*
- *change the management program*

- *redesign it*
- *put up a warning sign*
- *ignore it—stuff happens*
- *be more safe next time*

This list contains the most common favorite solution categories I have found over the years. It does not mean an effective solution is impossible if it comes from one of these categories. What it does say is that you are in a rut and chances are the problem will repeat itself. Favorite solutions usually mean you have also identified your favorite set of causes. Go back and look closer at the Realitychart. Look for branches, conditional causes, and causes between the causes. Chances are you missed some key branches or assumed a causal relationship that is not well understood.

Sometimes the solution may be to do nothing, for example, if the Realitychart reveals that the causes are unique and the probability of repeating is low. It may be that the consequences as identified in the significance portion of the problem definition are minimal. Again, always consider the solution criteria as a function of your purpose. The right answer is the one you choose as long as you can honestly say it meets the solution criteria.

The unthinkable may also happen. My studies show that in industry about 5 or 6% of the time we are not capable of finding a solution to our daily problems. This number seems to be consistent across different industries, and I believe the reason is that our knowledge of the processes we control is limited to about 95%. These statistics reflect the fact that sometimes we simply don't know what happened. This is not to say we won't know in time, but we stop looking because the task is too expensive, time consuming, or difficult. When we find ourselves in this condition, we should devise a plan to capture more information and causal evidence. If the problem happens again, we will know more causes.

Solution Killers

"A pessimist sees the difficulty in every opportunity; an optimist sees the opportunity in every difficulty." (Sir Winston Churchill)

Some people are simply not happy unless they are complaining about something. These chronic complainers see the world as one big problem; they are always complaining or putting others down. They are the only ones with the right answers and if the world would only stop long enough to ask their advice, everything would be wonderful. I suspect you work with some people like this and if you do you need to know how to overcome this negative attitude so the rest of the organization can accomplish effective solutions. Here is a short list of some common expressions used by these naysayers:

- *"It will never work here."*
- *"We're too busy for that."*
- *"No one will buy it."*
- *"We already tried that once."*
- *"That's not our policy here."*
- *"It isn't in the budget."*
- *"Good thought but impractical."*
- *"Top management will never go for it."*
- *"No one else is doing it that way."*
- *"Wrong!"*
- *"We've always done it that way."*
- *"Good idea, I'll get back with you"* (and never does).

Solution-killer statements are caused by the fear of change—the result of the natural process of continually validating our belief system. Some people are more affected by this than others. This process, I call "groovenation," meaning it creates a deep memory groove in our mind, starts in the teenage years, and all adults have it to varying degrees. Notice that children don't have this affliction. In fact they have exactly the opposite condition. They seek the unknown and welcome change as a gateway to experience, even at the risk of endangering themselves. If we can get the fearful people to be more like children and set aside their fears for a few minutes, they might be able to see other possibilities.

To do this, never let a solution-killer statement go unanswered, no matter who says it. This can be done tactfully by focusing on learning, growth, and improvement, not change. If the boss says a solution cannot be implemented because it is not in the budget, then redirect the focus to the purpose of doing business. Make sure you have done your homework and can show the ROI, the inherent value of the solution, or the requirement to fix the problem.

A common solution killer in business is related to money. I am amazed by how many middle-level managers do not understand that the purpose of business is to make money, not save it. Saving money is for governments and individuals on a fixed income. The rest of us are trying to make money. The fundamental process of doing business requires that you spend money to make money. If your solution can be shown to make money for the company, whether it is in the budget or not becomes a moot point. Any bank will lend money to an established business if they can show that the ROI is adequate. Look for other alternatives such as scheduling implementation over a longer period of time or until the money can be put in the budget, but do not let this solution-killer go unchallenged.

The purpose of the killer phrase is to stop discussion, and it works quite well if left unchallenged. If you are interested in effective solutions, it is imperative that you speak up. The best response is to ask the person making the statement to "say more about that." Pause, and if you don't get a response, ask another question like, "What do you mean we tried it once? Tell me what you did last time? Or, why did it fail?" Often, these people have no idea why the solution you are suggesting would fail. They will have opinions, but they will not have a cause-and-effect chart that documents the cause-and-effect relationships.

It often helps to play dumb; be the student and ask them to teach you, to explain why the solution will not work. As they provide answers, turn those answers into causes and see how they fit into the Realitychart. If they have valid concerns, they will fit into the common reality you are creating. In the process of adding their causes to the chart, you will have gained an ally. Your purpose in this strategy is not to prove the naysayers wrong. Your purpose is to get them to forget their fears long enough to play the game—to engage them in cause-and-effect thinking. By engaging them, you help them lose their fears and become confident with the new understanding they helped create. Once they see how well the process works, they become more open to it and will be more engaging thereafter.

Never get into an argument about who is right or who is wrong. There is no such thing in the world of events; the solutions are only good, better, or best. We never have enough information to totally understand anything we do; we can only operate on what we know. If it is documented on the Realitychart, at least we have a form of communication that allows for everyone's understanding to be represented. Obtaining this common reality is the key to effective problem solving, communication, and buy-in from all stakeholders.

Creative Solutions

Creativity and logic have always appeared at odds. They shouldn't be, but it is rare that a person is both very logical and creative. Like a flower, creativity can be nurtured and bloom or be nipped in the bud by the caregiver. The creative process is one of absurd connections, whereas the reasoning process is one of structure and rightness. Reasoning and creating seem to be on opposite ends of the mental spectrum, and indeed they cannot occur at the some point in time. This is not to say we can't jump from an analytic state of mind to a creative state in short order because we can, but the mere act of making absurd connections while laying out a clear set of logical connections may be impossible.

Regardless of the solution, creative or logical, we must understand the causal relationships between the solution and the primary effect; or we are back to guessing and voting, which have a low success rate. How can we go from one mental state to the other? Let's explore some strategies I have found to be very helpful.

Listen for the Laughter

Laughter is caused by the improbable connection of two or more things. "Of all the things I lost over the years, I think I miss my mind the most." If you find this funny, it is because you would never have thought of the possibility of losing your mind in the physical sense because it is secured between an impressive bone structure. It simply can't be lost. Yet we use "lost his mind" to describe people when they act strange. Since laughter and creativity both consist of heretofore unmade connections, it stands to reason that spontaneous laughter may lead us to creative solutions.

The next time you hear laughter while discussing solutions, stop and find out what caused the laughter. It usually appears to be something that is so absurd that you won't bother to take it any further. Do it anyway. Ask the person who caused the laughter to explain why doing whatever it was they suggested would have any effect on the problem. Don't ask them to explain why they thought of it and be very careful not to make any judgments. They may or may not be able to tell you why they said what they did, but look for a cause that is being removed, such as "fire the boss, yuk, yuk." You might ask what firing the boss would do? "Well, it would allow us to do our jobs right." "Does this mean we aren't doing our jobs right?" "How could we do them better?" "Are there barriers in the way?" As you go down this uncharted path, suspend judgment in a positive sense. That is, look at all statements as eventually leading to something positive, even if they initially appear not to.

Rapid Response Method

Another way to find creative solutions operates on the premise that since we cannot reason and create at the same time, we need to find a way to turn off the reasoning and only allow the absurd connections to come into our mind. Regardless of how creative people are, logic and reasoning usually creep back into the thought process. This is true except for the very creative, who have the ability to suspend all judgment and just go with their feelings. One way to force this activity is to not allow the mind time to analyze what is being presented. This requires a group of people and a facilitator who rapidly extracts ideas from the group, starting with the completed Realitychart. Use the following steps to find creative solutions.

Step 1: Create possible solutions.

Some call this step brainstorming, and it is in a way. However, it is different in that we are addressing a specific cause from the Realitychart, one cause at a time. This step requires the group to answer the question of what solution do you have that will remove, change, or control the cause being questioned. Before getting started, we need to establish some simple rules.

Rule #1: Speak only when it is your turn. The facilitator will let you know when it is your turn. No comments are allowed by anyone else for any reason during the creation session. If you have nothing to offer, you say "pass."

Rule #2: Do not explain your ideas. Again, that is an act of rationalizing. Put it on a bumper sticker and move on, quickly.

Rule #3: One solution at a time.

When I say work fast, I do mean fast. It may take two people writing to document the ideas because one cannot keep up and you don't want to slow down the group. If they slow down, they start thinking. The facilitator moves from one person to the next, focused on the cause you want to challenge until all participants have said "pass." Then move on to the next cause.

Step 2: Evaluate the effectiveness of the proposed solutions.

Go back and look at all the proposed solutions. Here, each person can explain their ideas as much as they want. Anyone can help the other person look for the connection if they have difficulty expressing it. When they hit on something interesting, the group begins to synergize. At this point, appreciatively understanding the other persons experience can help significantly. It is not unusual to discover your Realitychart, which was perfect a few minutes ago, is woefully inadequate at this point. Revise it as necessary.

If the group is tired from performing a causal analysis, it may be best to have the rapid response solution session some other time. Let problem significance guide you with respect to timing, how hard you work the group, and so forth.

The Gano Rule

Creativity often requires the use of what psychologists call the "unconscious mind." Using the unconscious mind is best accomplished by sleep and play. Unless time is critical, take as much time as you have to find the best solutions. After creating the Realitychart, sleep on it before you start the solutions phase. I have a rule that I always follow when making important decisions: I always sleep on it, unless I am forced to do otherwise. I call this the Gano Rule and salesmen don't like it. If you spend time trying different solutions and can't find any that really cause you to go wow!—sleep on it.

If you can't sleep, go play. Our unconscious mind is busy working on our problems while we play. Everyone has experienced the great aha's! that seem to come out of nowhere. The morning shower is a great place because the brain is usually not yet connected for the day; and we heat it up with hot water and the blood flows better, causing ideas to race through our minds. Sometimes those ideas seem strange, but they are simply new connections of thought. Evaluate after you get out of the shower, enjoy the moment of creativity, and write it down or try to explain it to your mate. This will help solidify it in the "real world."

Behavioral studies have shown that about 95% of all five-year-olds are highly creative, according to Charlie Palmgren of SynerChange International.[2] Then, something happens between the ages of five and eight. Less than 5% of those older than eight are highly creative. The research seems to indicate that formal education may be contributing to this lack of creativity. When children enter school, their learning goes from that of natural play to a structured, scheduled, and homogenized process based on the false premise that everyone is the same.

Failing to understand that play is the natural learning process, we force-feed children meaningless facts and rule-based schemes. If left to their own strategies, the child will solve problems by alternating between working on the problem and playing at something else. While the child is playing, the unconscious mind is working on the problem. When the child returns to the problem, the solution often just appears out of nowhere. As adults, you have probably experienced the same thing. Play is important to the natural problem-solving process, so we need to incorporate it into our problem-solving plan.

Yes-Anding

"Yes-anding" is a creative strategy that helps us avoid negative judgments throughout the solutions stage. It works like this. Avoid using the word "but." When a fellow team member says something you disagree with, try to empathize and then agree with it. Follow your profound agreement with the statement, "Yes, **and** we could add to that with [insert your idea.]" "Yes-anding" can be used to brainstorm by asking every person to build on the expressed solution. It moves very quickly, like the rapid response method, so we do not want to slow down the process with logic or analysis at this point. Be enthusiastic about the previous solution even if it is totally off the wall, such as, "Oh, *yes*! Wesley, that is the most incredible solution I have ever heard *and* we could build a miniature mousetrap from your new tennis racket by adding a spring at the bottom."

The "yes-and" strategy is based on what children do when they play. Young children have not yet learned to put each other down. They have no experience on which to judge, so they accept what is stated as being really cool and then build on the thought until they have turned a cardboard box into a castle complete with kitchen and cannons.

Identifying Effective Solutions

Effective solutions mean we must prevent the defined problem from happening again. If you are experiencing repeat events in your life or organization, you have missed the fundamental tenet of effective problem solving. Effective solutions are ones that work for you or your organization, not for someone else. A solution will work if it meets the criteria of preventing recurrence, is within your control, meets your goals and objectives, and doesn't cause other unacceptable problems.

The difference between conventional wisdom and the Reality-Charting problem-solving process is the belief in a right solution. As we have learned so far in this book, there is no such thing as one right answer to event-based problems, only good, better, and best. The best solutions not only meet the solution criteria, but they are the ones you or your organization choose. By involving key stakeholders in the problem-solving process, you will create a common reality from which effective solutions become obvious to all. If anyone else involved in the decision-making process has questions or doesn't understand the causes, they should be invited to add their reality to the chart so everyone can gain from their different perspective. When this happens, the solutions are more likely to be better. Removing the conflict found in most team-based problem-solving endeavors means effective solutions are more likely to get implemented because the stakeholders have ownership.

While the solutions are often more effective than other problem-solving processes, we need to be aware that a few people will not be willing to change their belief systems. As Henry Ford once said, "Whether you think you can or think you can't, you are right." By seeking to engage all perspectives and following the basic rules of the RealityCharting process, we can usually bring these naysayers into the fold and get effective solutions agreed to by all players.

Remember to listen for the laughter when considering solutions. There is always a smart aleck in every group, so listen for the telltale signs of laughter. Follow the reasons behind the laughter and look for the cause of the absurd connection. It is the creative solutions that are often the best solutions because they have identified a cause path that has never been understood before. As you become more and more proficient in using the RealityCharting process, you will experience some interesting interrelationships between problem definition, causes, significance, and solutions. They all seem to work off each other and since it is so easy to share the common reality and make changes with RealityCharting®, better solutions are more abundant.

To see how RealityCharting® makes it easy to add solutions and evaluate them against the solution criteria, go to http://coach.RealityCharting.com/Book/Wizard.

To practice adding solutions to a Realitychart, go to http://coach.RealityCharting.com/Book/Exercise5.2.

References

1. Rita Carter. *Mapping The Mind*. Los Angeles, University of California Press (1999).
2. Private communication from Charlie Palmgren, SynerChange International, Atlanta, Georgia.

10

Step Seven: Implement and Track Solutions

Genius is the ability to put into effect what is on your mind.

—F. Scott Fitzgerald

If after all the work of finding effective solutions we do not implement them and track them to verify their effectiveness, all our work is for naught, yet that is exactly what most organizations do. Success is not coming up with a good idea, it is bringing it to fruition in a way that provides the value. This chapter provides some guidelines on how to overcome the common pitfalls of implementing solutions.

Implementing solutions should be the easiest part of the process, but in fact most organizations fail miserably at this point. More than half the organizations that we have provided root cause analysis training to do not have a formal action tracking program. They rely on the integrity of the individual who was assigned the task to implement it. Even those organizations that have a formal corrective action tracking system fail to implement or follow through on solutions. It is common practice in many government organizations to have thousands of outstanding corrective actions waiting for disposition. And many of those that are attended to are implemented by using sleight-of-hand and storytelling to rationalize not doing anything. When the event occurs again, it is added to the statistical count then management is told that we still have a 50% failure rate, but that's what it has always been so it must be okay.

By providing a legitimate causal analysis defined in the Realitychart, it is much harder to ignore or rationalize not implementing the solutions. Furthermore, because all stakeholders can easily participate in the development of the chart and the solutions, they are more likely to buy into their implementation.

Corrective Actions Tracking Program

Using a master list, each corrective action should be documented in a log. The log should include the responsible person(s), completion date, and a brief description of the required action, with reference to more details and the Realitychart.

The corrective actions tracking log should be updated frequently and should have the highest visibility in the organization. The facility manager or similar authority should review the log weekly or more often if necessary. If a corrective action is not completed on time, an explanation must be provided and a new date assigned. Failure to maintain discipline on this list will be seen as a lack of commitment by management and the entire program will fail.

Corrective actions should be agreed to and approved by those who have the authority and responsibility to implement them—no one else.

Create a separate list for actions that call for review, analysis, or investigation. Long-term projects or "nice-to-do" tasks should be kept separate from the master corrective actions tracking log. The master log should only include those specific items that result from a formal investigation. Specifically, corrective actions are those derived from an event significant enough to require a formal investigation and that meet the four criteria for an effective solution (prevent recurrence, be within our control, meet our goals and objectives, and not cause other problems).

Trending Causes

Today, trending causes and problems is used to help us determine where best to put our resources to realize maximum benefit. Historically, trending has required categorization, but with the use of RealityCharting® and word search capabilities, the need for categorization diminishes. RealityCharting® has a "Find" feature that allows you to search for specific causes or specific causal elements so you can search your past Realitycharts to identify common repeatable causes, which in turn can help identify systemic causes/problems. Look for trending improvements in future releases of RealityCharting®.

If you are still using the old method of categorizing problems or causes and then creating a Pareto chart or other trending information, you need to remember that everyone categorizes differently. In many event reports, you may find a set of cause categories on a form that the individual is asked to check. These categories are then tracked and trended and compared. The National Safety Council has been gathering safety data on incidents this way since its inception. What they fail to understand is that because each person has a different perception of the world, each has a different categorization scheme. What one person understands to be a personnel error another person will see as a hardware or procedural failure.

For years I ran an exercise in my training courses where I would ask the students to categorize a list of thirty items into people, procedure, or hardware. We would then compare each item. To everyone's amazement, people would categorize many things differently. Some items are easily agreed upon, but others are not. An interesting thing about this exercise was the incredulity expressed by the students. Because of our fundamental belief that there is a single reality and that everyone can see it, it comes as a shock when we see an example of different realities. As an example, one item given in the exercise was "patience." Some categorized this as "people" because it is a characteristic of people. Others saw this as a "procedure" because it is a practiced strategy.

The lesson in this is that if you are going to trend causes by using categories, funnel all categorization through one or two like-minded people. This is not a question of what the "right" category is, but one of ensuring consistency. All databases that rely on checklist input from different people are subject to this same discrepancy, and therefore most databases provide bogus information.

While trending causes or problems is an essential element of conventional quality programs today, I submit that it is an ineffective methodology. The accepted purpose of trending problems or causes is the belief that we can make a first cut in the vast problems we have and only focus on the top 20% that cause 80% of the losses. While this is a valid statistical approach, it is based on the assumption that repeat events are the norm. If you are having repeat events, it either means you have an ineffective problem-solving program or the events are not important enough to warrant your attention.

Organizations that have implemented the RealityCharting method do not have repeat events, so the need for tracking and trending causes becomes a moot point. If the problems are not significant enough for us to prevent, we should not waste time tracking and trending them.

The key here is to work on all significant problems as defined by some threshold criteria that you establish. As the total number of problems becomes smaller because they do not recur; lower your threshold criteria to work on less significant problems. This is what continuous improvement is all about.

Bear in mind that until such time as you have fully implemented the RealityCharting problem-solving program, you will need to work with your existing trending program. After you work the problems off the current list, all you will need to do is track the total number of events exceeding the threshold criteria. The total number will provide a gauge to help you decide when to lower your threshold criteria.

11

Effective Problem-Solving Culture

It's a funny thing about life: If you refuse to accept anything but the very best, you very often get it.

—Somerset Maugham

We have been teaching a form of root cause analysis to industry for over twenty years and we found that while we have trained over 100,000 people in over 2,000 companies in seven major languages, we have never seen any organizations that have been able to instill an effective problem-solving culture. To help us better understand the causes of this, we performed our own analysis using the RealityCharting® software and found many causes, only some of which we have control of. It took fifteen months and a little help from our friends to develop solutions to help organizations create an effective problem-solving culture. What we need is a program that shows inherent value simply by using it. In this way, all stakeholders will see the value and want to implement it. Effective problem solving then becomes institutionalized as a way of thinking, not as an appurtenance or new "program of the month."

This chapter lays out the basic elements of an effective program centered around the RealityCharting process.

The success of every organization is dependent on the people and the strategies they use to accomplish their goals. Perhaps one of the most important strategies needed for success is an effective problem-solving process. In his book, *How the Mighty Fall*, Jim Collins points to hubris as one of the main factors in the failure of great companies. Since hubris is pride or greed, people with this trait are driven by arrogance to think they know better than the next person. It is not surprising that hubris is a failure factor because most people think they are already good problem solvers and don't need any help. To overcome or prevent this hubris, we suggest you watch the Effective Problem Solving video at http://Coach. RealityCharting.com/book/Effective-Problem-Solving.

This should be viewed by everyone in your organization, including top-level managers, whose job includes some kind of problem-solving because it will help them understand the complexity of causal relationships and the principles that govern reality. For additional information read A Brief History and Critique of Causation at http://Coach.RealityCharting. com/book/Brief-History.

Start at the Bottom

In most organizations, problem solving is relegated to a few people, such as managers, supervisors, or subject matter experts such as engineers, programmers, designers, etc. Because most big problems are caused by small problems, preventing recurrence of the small problems should be a high priority for every business. However, since most people are not good problem solvers, and there are too many small problems for the designated problem solvers to tackle, stuff happens. To remedy this situation, we have created RealityCharting Simplified™ software, which anyone can use on any event-type problem and obtain a good understanding of the causes behind the problem. This is a free application that should be made available to everyone who has to solve problems as part of their normal business activities. It includes three very informative training videos that everyone should watch. It should also be incorporated into all procedures related to identifying and correcting deficiencies. A hidden benefit of using RealityCharting Simplified™ is that it teaches the user to think causally. People learn that stuff does not just happen and that by understanding causal relationships they can prevent problems from happening in the first place. To learn more go to http:// www.realitycharting.com/realitycharting/simplified.

Strengthen the Middle

Effective problem solving should include all stakeholders, but most problem-solving processes do not accommodate different perspectives very well and we waste a lot of time trying to convince others of the validity of our perspective. To overcome this significant problem, use RealityCharting® software to facilitate the problem-solving process and create a common reality that all stakeholders can buy into. All managers and supervisors whose job requires them to solve event-type problems should learn how to use RealityCharting® so they can effectively communicate the causal relationships of a given event. Please note that RealityCharting® can also be used to document the causes of your successes, so all stakeholders can know how to repeat them. Learning the RealityCharting process has never been easier. We have created an online learning module found in step 3 of the RealityCharting Learning Center. To learn more, go to http://coach.realitycharting.com.

With the purchase of RealityCharting® software, anyone can learn the process in four to six hours. To hone your skills and learn more in-depth knowledge about effective problem solving, the RealityCharting Learning Center provides a facilitation simulator and a library full of very helpful articles such as how to conduct interviews, or find the best evidence.

The key to making this part of your comprehensive plan work is to designate one or more problem-solving champions whose primary job is to facilitate investigations by creating a Realitychart for all major incidents *and* to promote causal thinking throughout the organization by teaching and reviewing the work of others. You will need to establish certified incident investigators who are first certified by a designated consultant and then promoted from within using a mentoring process. The mentoring should include the prospective facilitators watching an experienced facilitator and working their way up to performing an acceptable analysis on their own—being guided and mentored by the certified facilitator.

Promotion from the Top

Our experience shows that once managers see the incredible return on investment from using the RealityCharting process, they demand to see a Realitychart for all significant events. By establishing threshold criteria for when to perform a formal investigation, resources are effectively managed and problems are prevented from recurring. Because problems do not recur and more are being discovered and resolved using RealityCharting

Simplified™, the threshold for formal investigations is gradually lowered over time, thus improving efficiency and increasing the bottom line.

Management can easily buy into this plan because all the training is free and the RealityCharting® software itself is very economically priced. And being readily available online, there are few deployment issues to work out. By creating a culture where everyone in the organization understands the principles of causation and the key steps to effective problem solving, you will enjoy the success of your hard work and avoid the pain of failure.

Commitment to Continuous Improvement

To exist is to understand the here and now; to grow and prosper requires a commitment to learning. A fundamental tenet of the quality movement since W. Edwards Deming, the renowned quality management consultant, continuous improvement is much harder to do than to say. As we learned in chapter one, the human mind is designed to establish patterns that cause success, and once we find a success path it is hard to change. We simply do not like change of any kind. It is only the few, who actually experience the value of change, who understand this concept.

The willingness to change is a lesser force than the need to maintain status quo. I saw this in action when I helped conduct a review of a corporate safety audit at one of our client's plants. We were trying to find the causes of a significant breakdown in the safety program. Along the way we found many causes, but as the review continued, I began to notice increasing evidence of a failure to learn from mistakes. In fact, I noticed a total lack of respect for learning. This facility had a proud history of being number one in the corporation when it came to safety. Having succeeded, they came to believe they had a formula for success and could ride on that formula forever.

As environmental laws changed and new safety requirements were implemented, this organization wrote procedure after procedure to accommodate the new requirements, but little actually changed. When asked how they knew that laws and standards were being implemented, every department head said because it was in the *Safety and Health Manual*. After I repeated the questions a few more times, they all admitted they had no idea how they met all the requirements set forth in the manual. Indeed, many of the requirements were not being met. An internal audit had revealed their noncompliance and it was ignored for almost a year until their corporate audit team arrived onsite. Groovenation rules!

Learning requires a questioning attitude. Without a questioning attitude we fall into the human trap of groovenation, where our minds seek the familiar and reject anything new or different from our existing paradigms. Another investigator and I witnessed this as we were leaving the plant following the review. On the way out we passed two fire hydrants near the cafeteria. Both were rusted, but one had a severely bent box wrench hanging on the side. This wrench opens the valve to supply of water to fight fires when needed. We stopped to ponder the implications in light of the Realitychart we had just finished. The hydrant was one more piece of evidence of the causes we had found, but more fundamentally, it exemplified the lack of a questioning attitude. We wondered out loud how many other conditional causes lay in wait of an action to cause significant consequences. As the workers walked by this condition each day, they saw nothing.

We looked at it with fresh eyes and asked what caused a forged wrench to be so severely bent? Could it be a sticky valve that may not open when needed? Whatever the cause, it is clearly beyond the design basis of the wrench, yet it goes unnoticed. Why?

What I found, which is common to most companies and industries today, is a corporate policy that advocates a commitment to continuous learning yet punishes or derides anyone who speaks up about potential problems. What we must ask is why these seemingly intelligent people do this. Certainly, the cause has to do with group dynamics and the notion of a collective consciousness whereby we suspend our individuality for the perceived benefit of the group, but I think it is more than this. In organizations where effective leadership exists, they do not have this problem, so I believe a deeper cause is the inability of the leadership to deal with questioning attitudes.

Effective leaders understand the value of a questioning attitude and incorporate strategies to encourage it. However, it has been my experience that effective leaders do not grow on trees and most managers and so-called leaders simply do not possess the skills to resolve different perspectives. Quite often, the management strategy is "my way or the highway." For a concise, but detailed discussion on management styles and processes go to http://coach.RealityCharting.com/book/management.

The Realitychart can be used to change this inability to deal with conflicting ideas and perspectives. By providing a simple tool that allows for all perspectives to be viewed in one picture, different realities can be discussed in an argument-free environment. By communicating with evidence-based causes, we eliminate ineffective storytelling and inference by categorization. We replace these old strategies with a simple tool that encourages a questioning attitude and differences of opinion.

Another example of the difficulty of continuous improvement was demonstrated to me personally when I sent a paper about the RealityCharting process for publication in a quality assurance trade magazine. After months of review by the peer review committee, I was told this method was not root cause analysis because it did not include the popular Ishikawa fishbone diagram, which is the foundation of problem solving in many quality assurance programs.

The reviewers had established a fixed view of the world and were not going to be "misled" by anything new. Yet these same people are the ones espousing continuous improvement. This is not personal failure on their part, but rather part of a greater tragedy of the human condition caused by the natural tendency toward biased thought. The majority of us simply can't help ourselves. It seems to be fundamental to the nature of the organism.

To help your organizations break out of this trap, a learning environment must be established. At the heart of this environment is a new way of communicating that uses the Realitychart as the basis for decisions; however, a new philosophy also must be established that is based on the need for improvement. By focusing on improvement, not change, people are more likely to accept change.

Educating employees about the cause-and-effect principle will help them learn that things do not just happen. Everything has a cause and only our ignorance prevents us from knowing the causes. By knowing that every effect has conditional and action causes, they begin to see all the conditional causes around them and wonder what action cause will come along and cause an undesirable effect. Or, what action they can take that will combine with the conditional causes they observe to cause the desirable effect they seek.

By understanding that there is an infinite set of causes, again limited only by our own ignorance, we can begin to overcome the arrogance associated with right-minded thinking—thinking that has been shoved at us all our lives by various institutions that we established to "educate" us.

With a firm understanding of the cause-and-effect principle, a philosophy that values everyone's perspective is possible. From this philosophy comes the understanding that continuous improvement is not only possible but is the best course of action. We can let go of our fear of change and seek the unknown with the full knowledge that the infinite nature of the cause-and-effect principle will allow and encourage effective problem solving.

Institutionalizing the Process

As a working engineer, I was called upon to solve many technical problems. I can remember my fear each time I was called. I was well trained to know the laws of physics and how they applied to daily life and the industry in which I worked, yet I was always anxious. My anxiety was always based on the fear I would not have the right specific knowledge to solve the problem.

After internalizing the cause-and-effect principle and recognizing the infinite possibilities for solving any problem, the anxiety is gone and I now attack all problems without fear of failure. While I know I don't know what the causes or solutions will be, I do know that I can take the expertise of those who work on the problem and create a Realitychart to find the best solutions every time. With each success and no failures, the need to cling to a fixed set of rules and prejudices falls away. A sense of freedom replaces the fear of failure. The diversity of others' thoughts becomes the pieces of a common reality that enables learning.

Institutionalization of effective problem solving is best obtained by following the guidelines listed earlier. For a direct link to this information, go to http://www.realitycharting.com/training/rc-training/problem-solving-culture.

RealityCharting Simplified™ is available to everyone to perform a first-cut analysis of the problems they encounter and, if significant, they can easily pass the analysis to their supervisor who has a full version of RealityCharting® where a much more thorough analysis can be performed. RealityCharting® is used to document and share findings with all stakeholders. As time goes by, stakeholders eventually have a very good representation of the causes of their problem and can then effect changes to prevent recurrence. The tools are simple enough to be used by anyone on any problem and at any location.

Prior to spending money, most companies want evidence that their expenditures will provide a significant Return On Investment (ROI). Each problem is different and while I can recite examples that have earned companies millions of dollars on one problem, the average ROI for problems solved using RealityCharting® is 3,500% or approximately $25,000 within the first month. This figure is for manufacturing and process industries and does not account for repeated successes, which directly multiply this ROI. Similar successes occur in safety, quality, and service-related problems, but it is harder to assess actual dollars earned.

Among the many cases of payback, one I have tracked for several years comes to mind. Using the RealityCharting process for the first time, a reliability engineer was rewarded by fixing an old problem. He started his investigation with a piece of equipment that had failed thirty-five times in its lifetime. It had failed twelve times during the previous year. He assembled a team, gathered information, and prepared a Realitychart. Within a few days, the team had developed a new understanding of the problem from the common reality of the cause-and-effect chart. The solutions they implemented prevented recurrence.

When I spoke to him ten months after the corrective actions were implemented, there had not been a single failure. Three years later, they have still not had a failure. Since previous failures cost a minimum of $15,000 each, correcting this one problem has saved hundreds of thousands of dollars. He continues to use the RealityCharting process to drive his problem solving and continues to have successes like this one. Prior to learning the RealityCharting process, he had been using the conventional methods discussed in chapter two. These methods simply don't work because they don't follow the cause-and-effect principle.

When to Perform an Analysis

In every organization an incident investigation policy should be established to determine when a Realitychart should be created, and everyone should understand and buy into the policy. I have found three basic elements make it work: threshold criteria, evidence preservation policy, and clearly defined responsibilities.

Threshold Criteria

When we set about to establish a structured problem-solving process, the inevitable question arises: When should an investigation be performed? The simple answer is whenever you encounter unacceptable consequences. After implementing the RealityCharting process, this question becomes less important because trained employees will adopt

RealityCharting as a routine part of their job. The question then becomes when do we need to document the analysis process? Every organization needs to establish its own threshold criteria or sentinel events to answer this question. These criteria are a function of the industry and the organization. A service company will have threshold criteria such as "customer complaint" or "missed a goal." Manufacturers will have criteria like "total cost greater then $10,000" or "mean time between repair less than one year." Government organizations that enforce standards and laws have a ready set of criteria and only need to refer to any discrepancies or violations.

If an organization is properly using the RealityCharting process, there will be no more repeat events. Therefore, the number of events reaching the threshold criteria will eventually go to zero. Long before this happens, the criteria should be revised. In keeping with the spirit of continuous improvement, the threshold criteria should be periodically reviewed and revised to match the time available to perform investigations. If the time spent on investigation exceeds the time needed to operate the business, then the criterion is way too tight—relax it. If, on the other hand, no problems are meeting the threshold criteria, tighten them up. This periodic review must be part of an incident investigation program.

Evidence Preservation Policy

Establish a policy that requires preserving evidence. For example, broken equipment should be quarantined until experts can examine it and gather data. All too often in manufacturing and process plants, a piece of equipment breaks and because the organization is so efficient at fixing broken parts, a new one is installed and the old part discarded before anyone else knows of the failure. The same thing occurs in service industries when problems go unreported. Customer complaints are resolved, but no analysis is performed to find out why the problem occurred.

The efficiency at fixing broken parts is born out of the preventive maintenance or "broke-fix" mindset of the past. If we focus on reliability rather than repair, there will be no repair unless it provides the most cost-effective option. With this perspective, all failures are understood and measures are taken to prevent them, such as by replacing critical components before they fail or running noncritical components until they fail. This perspective also includes creating a Realitychart on all unexpected failures, which requires preserving evidence.

Use an evidence preservation checklist (discussed in chapter twelve) to obtain all relevant data, including personnel statements. Having a plan to gather as much information as possible immediately after the event is equally important. Identifying key people and giving them the responsibility to gather data as soon as possible can mean the difference between knowing the cause and the big shrug that occurs when the cause isn't known.

Responsibilities Defined

Establish committed investigation personnel to be on call twenty-four hours a day if your operation runs all day. They should start gathering data as soon as all safety issues have been dealt with. These people can be properly trained shift personnel or employees living nearby. A single individual should be given the responsibility to start gathering data and to make sure all others are doing their assigned tasks. Everyone and anyone should be available to help if the event meets one of the threshold criteria. If there is no commitment here, then the threshold criteria may be too low. That is, if the problem does not warrant the time to find out how to prevent recurrence, then maybe it should not be worked on. Again, this is part of the questioning attitude needed for continuous learning.

Simple Reporting Scheme

A formal incident report should contain the following information, at a minimum:

1. Problem Definition
    What
    When
    Where
    Significance
       Loss
       Frequency
       Safety Issue
2. Summary Statement
3. Corrective Actions and Associated Causes
4. Responsible Person and Completion Date
5. Cost Information or ROI

6. Contact Person
7. Report Date

Keep the report simple. As Albert Einstein reportedly said, "If you can't say it simply, you probably don't understand it." As a young supervisor, I used to get so many long-winded reports on my desk that I used the manage-by-reputation method to review them. I would read the subject, the summary (if provided), and who wrote the report. If it was written by someone I knew and trusted to do a good job, I often just approved it. There wasn't enough time in the day to adequately read all reports, let alone gain an appreciative understanding of them. When you consider my strategy (not uncommon today) and the fact that only 30% of the workforce are effective problem solvers, it is no wonder that problems kept happening. The report should be limited to one page and have a Realitychart attached.

The information contained in the Realitychart is more important than the form. The report could contain more information than given here, but these items have proven effective in providing enough information to communicate the event and ensure that effective problem solving will occur. You should always create your own form to meet your needs. Do not encourage restrictive thinking by including endless checklists and specific questions such as, "Was the hazardous condition recognized?" These only serve to limit thinking and foster favorite solutions that will ensure a repeat event.

The summary statement is simply verbiage that reflects the core set of causes in the attached Realitychart. The purpose of the summary statement is more to meet traditional expectations than provide any real value. Since the Realitychart provides everything one needs to understand the causes and effectiveness of the solutions, the summary statement is somewhat redundant. However, in its defense, I have found that many traditional managers are unwilling to accept such a radical change as to provide only a Realitychart, so I suggest the summary statement be included in the interest of harmony when dealing with Luddites.

Final Note

The RealityCharting process is simple and easy to use, but as we saw in chapter one, it is in conflict with what we normally do. To overcome our natural tendencies to tell stories and communicate categorically, people need to understand how ineffective current problem solving is and how effective it can be. To help them shift their paradigm from their current ineffective strategies, have them watch the Effective Problem Solving video at http://Coach.RealityCharting.com/book/Effective-Problem-Solving.

An honest dedication to continuous improvement is now possible because the Realitychart provides a simple tool to accommodate differences in perception. A questioning environment is now encouraged. Indeed, it is embraced by those who once could not deal with dissension. The common reality created by the Realitychart enables individuals and organizations to more easily follow the dictum of continuous improvement.

By using the RealityCharting process and establishing some threshold criteria that dictate when to perform formal incident investigations, we can break out of the useless policy of trending repeat events and focus on prevention instead.

The key to making an effective problem-solving program work is to have a dedicated champion for every business unit. The dedicated champion must be experienced, affable, and respected by most people in the organization. The champion should report at the highest level in the business unit and have the ability to cross all organizational boundaries. The champion is someone who is not only well versed in the RealityCharting process, but who also teaches as he or she promotes the concepts and uses RealityCharting® to communicate all problem-solving matters. The champion is often the one who is called on to facilitate the investigation of major events. As such, the champion must have special skills in group facilitation. These skills are discussed in the next chapter.

12

Facilitation Skills

Working together to accomplish great things will always
be a part of the human experience and success depends on
our people skills and individual courage to confront group
consensus.

—Irving Janis

Effective problem solving can be accomplished individually or in a group. The RealityCharting method will work in either situation, but the most powerful is with a group of knowledgeable players. A group without a leader is a mob, and a problem-solving team without a skilled facilitator is just another group. Therefore, it is imperative that you have a skilled facilitator. The RealityCharting Learning Center at http://www.realitycharting.com/facilitations/arm-broken provides a facilitation simulator to help you gain confidence in using the software. The following information will help you with the soft skills of facilitation.

Do not confuse group facilitation, a recognized field unto itself, with facilitating the creation of a Realitychart. While facilitating skills are very helpful in creating a good Realitychart, the guidelines in this chapter are more specific to facilitating the RealityCharting problem-solving process.

A good facilitator does not have to know anything about the problem. It is often a major benefit for the facilitator to know nothing about the problem as long as they know how to gather information and use RealityCharting®.

Facilitating is a process of gathering information, defining the problem, creating a Realitychart, and finding creative effective solutions while practicing appreciative understanding.

Facilitating the problem-solving process can be significantly enhanced if the facilitator has good people skills. This chapter is designed to provide some guidance in this area and address many of the problems encountered during facilitation. We will also discuss several ineffective human strategies and how to overcome them. The final section provides some common questions and answers that I hope are helpful.

Facilitation Guidelines

The purpose of the facilitator is to ease and promote the problem-solving process. The problem-solving process generally follows the sequence of gathering information, defining the problem, creating a Realitychart, and identifying solutions, with the caveats that gathering information occurs throughout the process and problem definition can change at anytime. The following guidelines are provided to help facilitators with each of these steps. Because a key aspect of gathering information involves interviewing, that subject is also covered in detail.

Gather Information

While listed as the first step, gathering information is a continual process starting with finding out everything you can about an event and continuing until you verify that the solution meets the three criteria. Gathering information is not an individual task. Everyone in the organization should be trained and understand the need for causes and evidence. As a minimum they should watch the Effective Problem Solving video at http://Coach.RealityCharting.com/book/Effective-Problem-Solving.

This will significantly enhance the efficiency of the investigation because it teaches what is expected of the participants.

Appreciative understanding plays a big role in every part of effective problem solving, but it plays a crucial role when gathering information. Any parochial judgments or biases used to filter or eliminate information at this stage may prove very damaging to your success later on—do not discard anything in the initial discovery phase.

Timeliness is the essence of success when gathering information. Evidence preservation policies should be established, known by everyone, and used assiduously. In manufacturing facilities, an overzealous focus on production often gets in the way of evidence gathering. If we do not take the time to gather evidence on significant problems, chances are they may not be solved.

Tenacity and doggedness are key watchwords in any investigation. Consider the following story of the payoffs it can bring. In 1926 one of the largest producers of tool steel in the United States provided the auto industry with most of its critical components. About this time the number of auto accidents began to rise and drivers were being killed when steering knuckles began to fail. We tend to believe that our problems are caused by others and the automakers were no exception. They immediately blamed the steel company for providing inferior steel. The steel companies checked every possible cause at their end and could find nothing. The steel tested correctly and nothing changed during shipment to the automakers. When the automakers gave the steel company an ultimatum to correct this unknown problem an engineer from the steel company was sent to Detroit to observe the automakers use of the steel. All processes were checked and nothing was discovered to suggest any problems. The heating temperatures where checked and were found to be exact, but the problem persisted. Being tenacious by nature this engineer decided to have the temperature gauges checked. He found that the same company manufactures all of the gauges and indeed they were all found to be faulty. The end result was that while the steel was being made into steering knuckles it was heated by several hundred degrees higher than it should have been. The problem was solved and steering knuckles did not present a problem again—until recently when the same problem occurred with another US car maker. In addition to the need to be tenacious, an added lesson here is to validate your inferred evidence when things don't seem right.

Preserve evidence by securing the environment, the people, and the process controls. If dealing with broken hardware, do not touch the broken parts and get them to your material specialist as soon as possible. Limit access to the area or equipment, find out who was involved, and what they know about the event. If process controls such as procedures are involved, identify them and their role in the event. It is often helpful to have a "go-bag" on hand to help in the information-gathering process. A typical investigator's go-bag consists of the following items (make your own list):

- *digital camera*
- *paper and pencils*
- *interview guidelines*
- *evidence preservation checklist*
- *other guidelines*
- *grid paper for mapping*
- *measuring tape*
- *flashlight*
- *labels, tags, and duct tape*
- *steel ruler*
- *feeler gauges*
- *marking pens*
- *sealable plastic bags*
- *small voice recorder for your notes*
- *magnifying glass*
- *magnet*
- *rags*
- *sample bottle(s)*
- *why questions—a questioning attitude*
- *inspection mirror*

Guidance in gathering evidence can be obtained from a reference list called the "evidence preservation checklist." A typical industry checklist follows, but you should create your own:

- *Preserve the condition and location of hardware*
- *Equipment*
- *Tools*
- *Materials (removed or installed)*
- *Obtain and preserve documentation*
- *Regulations and standards*
- *Procedures*
- *Work instructions*
- *Design drawings*
- *Operator logs*

- Equipment logs
- Process strip charts
- Work requests
- Maintenance records
- Surveillance records
- Quality records
- Work schedules
- Computer printouts
- Document evidence
- Photos, sketches, drawings, and maps
- Collect input
- Personnel statements
- Interviews or peer review reports

Based on the initial information and problem definition, determine who will be involved in the problem-solving team. This may change as the need for expert advice is realized. Only invite people who will contribute to the effort. Caution: Limit the number of people in the team to fewer than eight. Four or five is optimal for most events. With a very complicated problem, you may want to create multiple teams to address special areas. These teams should report to the main team by providing their portion of the Realitychart. Always maintain a master Realitychart that everyone can look at anytime during the investigation.

Develop a sequence of events or timeline before you start to create a Realitychart. The sequence of events will provide an initial set of action causes that can be used to help you develop the initial chart.

RealityCharting® has a Wizard that helps you through the entire problem-solving process and it should be used by the experienced facilitator. If you are not an experienced facilitator, you should use the following guidelines until you gain the necessary confidence.

Define the Problem

After the initial information gathering, the team should come together with an overhead projector or online screen-sharing software with RealityCharting on the screen. Open the meeting with your expectations and set the following ground rules as applicable:

1. Everyone should strive to appreciatively understand all points of view.
2. Complaining, comparing, or competing is not allowed.

3. The purpose is to fix the problem, not to blame.
4. Everyone is here to contribute.
5. This is an open dialog; judging or stating conclusions are not allowed until the solutions phase.
6. We are not trying to find the right answer; we are going to find the best solutions.
7. We will not talk about solutions until after we create a Realitychart.
8. The best solutions must meet three criteria: prevent recurrence, be within our control, and meet our goals and objectives, to include not causing other problems and providing a reasonable return on investment.
9. Be patient with the process.
10. Do not hold side conversations.
11. We are looking for causes and their supporting evidence.
12. Everything is open to discussion, but the facilitator reserves the right to direct the discussion to follow evidence-based causes.
13. Assumptions are encouraged, and they will be labeled with a question mark until we can find supporting evidence.

Begin to define the problem by asking the team members to identify the primary effect as they see it. Write each one down. As taught in RealityCharting Coach this will generate many causes, so use the brainstorming tool to input every cause you hear. You will have to trick RealityCharting "Wizard" into thinking you have defined the problem in order to get to the brainstorming feature, so just input a best guess at this point.

Listen for cause statements and write them down. Record every notable cause statement by placing it on the chart or in the holding area using the brainstorming feature. (You may want to delegate data input to another team member. This can free up the facilitator to focus on dealing with people who insist on telling stories.) Remember, don't judge whether these are primary effects or not, just input everything. People are providing their perspective and each cause is part of the puzzle.

When no further causes come, ask the team which cause they think is the primary effect and begin putting them in order from present to past. This will get you to a primary effect that most can agree on, so you can now go back and revise the problem definition.

After you have a general agreement on the primary effect, finish the problem statement by writing the when, where, and significance so everyone can see. Remember to provide specific information about safety, cost, and frequency.

Do not proceed with further chart development until every member agrees with the written problem statement. If you cannot get concurrence, remind dissenters that this can be changed anytime and ask if you can move on.

If there is more than one primary effect, write out a problem statement for each and then proceed to ask why of one primary effect at a time.

Create a Realitychart

Starting with the primary effect, begin asking "why?" or asking "caused by?" until you no longer get answers. Many answers will already be in front of you from the problem definition stage; use them.

Encourage an open dialogue. No one judges; if anyone does, remind them of the ground rules. It is not unusual to feel you have lost control at this stage. This is quite normal and can last twenty to thirty minutes. Each individual reality is pouring out and it is usually productive as long as everyone follows the ground rules. This is very similar to working on a jigsaw puzzle; things are not very clear until you get some pieces to fit together. It will come together. After experiencing this a few times, you gain confidence and recognize the out-of-control feeling as normal. Listen carefully and input every cause you hear without regard for where it fits into the puzzle; that will come later as you go through the Square One Loop.

Remember, causes are noun-verb phrases. Listen for them. To keep everyone interested, validate their ideas by inputting their causes and putting them on the chart. If the cause is valuable, it will fit; if it is not, it will fall away and everyone will see why. Do not waste time at this point trying to judge or evaluate the value of each offered cause.

Minimize discussion during this phase by asking why immediately after placing the cause on the chart. This important point keeps people focused and moving down a productive path. Anything you can do to keep moving prevents storytelling and gets you to a common reality much sooner. The facilitator can work on cleaning up the logic at a later date and then share with the team. Minimizing the drudgery of an investigation makes people want to do this again for other problems. Avoid getting bogged down in endless analysis and storytelling. The difference between a trained team and an untrained team can mean hours in problem resolution time. The well-trained team will come to the meeting with causes and evidence while the untrained team will come with stories and opinions. Everyone should receive some training in the RealityCharting problem-solving process. The time saved and the quality of the solutions justifies the time spent on training many times over.

Go back to the primary effect (Square One) and start through the cause chains again. Look for causes in actions and conditions. Caution: Do not let this become an obsession. The reason you are looking for actions and conditions is that the cause-and-effect principle dictates they are there; and the more causes you can find, the better your solutions.

Hint: If you have an action cause and can't find a condition you can often create a condition by taking the noun in the action cause and adding the word "exists" to it. For example, if the action cause is "Ignored Work Signs" a conditional cause is "Work Signs Exist." If you have a conditional cause and are having difficulty finding an action cause look for words that end in –ed. This does not always produce a verb (action), but will help most of the time. For example if your effect is "Potential Electrical Contact" and a conditional cause is "Hands Near Electricity" the action cause could be "Electrical Circuits Activated," as opposed to "Electrical Circuits Active."

Ideas and causes are usually coming so fast on the first pass it is better to keep the momentum going than to slow down the thought process by labeling causes. As you go through the second and subsequent loops, look for the needed action or condition and baby steps. If you can't find the needed action or condition, don't worry about it.

Go to your point of ignorance. Repeat the Square One Loop as many times as needed to get question marks or make a decision to stop at the end of each cause chain.

In addition to looking for the actions and conditions, you need to make sure each causal element is valid and complete. To ensure the validity, run the Advanced Rules Checks for Space-Time and Causal Logic. You should also ask if there are any other causes required to cause the effect in question. To help jog your mind, ask if there are other causes that mitigated or exacerbated the effect. Look very carefully at each causal element to ensure you have found all the necessary causes.

If you do not want to go further, then stop and identify solutions. Normally you will need to gather more information to find answers to several why questions and to find supporting evidence. Remember, RealityCharting® will create an action item report for you if there is a question mark in the evidence box, which is the default condition, and More Information Needed is given as an end point in a cause chain. Assign responsibilities in the action item report and send it to all responsible players. Decide when to reconvene, and dismiss the team until then.

While evidence can be added at anytime as you go through the Realitychart, it is often best to wait until after you have most causes identified. If evidence is not available, develop a plan to obtain the supporting data.

Complete the Realitychart as best you can. Remember it is impossible to know all the causes. Problem significance will help you to know how far to go with baby steps or termination of the cause chains. Time constraints may also limit exploration, but don't dwell on this. Your purpose is to find a creative solution that meets your goals and objectives and if you accomplish that then you have accomplished what you set out to do. When you get to the solutions stage and you cannot find an effective solution, then work on the chart some more. This is common.

If storytelling erupts, let it go as long as you are getting causes out of the story. As soon as it digresses into who did what at such-and-such a time at such-and-such a place, stop it and get back into the Square One Loop.

Make sure not to stop too soon on each cause path. Before you decide to stop, look at the last cause in each cause path and try to ask why two more times. If you end up in "la-la land," then you know you went too far. If you get good answers, keep going. The most common tendency is to stop at categorical causes like "Training Less Than Adequate," or "Maintenance Less Than Adequate." Another common stopping point is "Procedures Not Followed." These are categories, not causes, and they must be explained in more detail. Sometimes it helps to ask, "What do you mean by 'less than adequate' or 'not followed'"?

Refrain from discussing solutions and root causes while you are constructing the Realitychart.

Identify Solutions

Once you have decided to stop adding causes to your chart and you have completed Wizard Step 2 in RealityCharting®, either print the chart or use an overhead screen and begin to brainstorm solutions with all key stakeholders. This can be done electronically or in a meeting. The meeting forum works best because it allows for synergy. Select Wizard Step 3 and brainstorm solutions.

As you challenge each cause, provide solutions. RealityCharting® provides two easy ways to do this. You can either select Wizard Step 3, Create Solutions, and it will take you through each cause on the chart in a structured way, or you can use the Solutions Tool (light bulb at the top of the work space), which will allow you to add solutions to any cause you click on. Do not be concerned about strict compliance with the solution criteria at this time. RealityCharting® will help you do this later. This is similar to brainstorming in the sense that you should allow unbiased free thought. Get all team members involved in the creative solutions process to build ownership.

Hint: As you gain experience with the RealityCharting process, you will find the solution criteria are part of your thinking as you consider each cause. While it should not restrict your thinking, it acts as a guide to keep you focused on a solution that prevents recurrence, is within your control, and meets your goals.

Continue challenging the causes. Do not waste time with causes that do not offer good solutions. If no one in the group can think of anything, move on. Normally, this should not take more than twenty minutes as a group activity. If you have time, it is a good idea to let the solutions "cook" for some time. Talk with people outside the group about the proposed solutions or go to the place where the solution will be implemented and try to visualize implementation. This often identifies other problems.

After identifying solutions, check each one against the solution criteria and decide on the best ones. They must meet the criteria, which include not causing other problems and providing good value for your investment.

You may find one solution that will prevent the problem from happening "most of the time." As you affect more causes and add more solutions, you are reducing the probability of a repeat event, but there comes a point of diminishing returns. Only you can decide where that is, based on your goals and objectives.

Some solutions may not prevent the stated problem from recurring but will help create a better environment for success and therefore may warrant implementation.

Be very careful not to stop with your favorite solution or a group consensus that compromises the effectiveness of better solutions.

After you have entered all your possible solutions, use RealityCharting® to verify compliance with the solution criteria or not. Select which solutions you plan to implement and then finish up the report using Wizard Steps 4 and 5.

Send the finalized report to all stakeholders for review and approval. If you get comments at this stage, remember that you do not have to be defensive about what you created. If someone has new perspectives and evidence based-causes to add, put them on the chart—it is easy to do so and they may lead to better solutions. One of the greatest values of using the RealityCharting problem-solving process is that its core value is to create a common reality that everyone can understand and buy into. By its very nature, creating a common reality in your Realitychart assures the best solutions.

Conducting Interviews

When gathering information from people, effective interviewing skills can make all the difference. While it is best to get people with the knowledge of the problem into the team that is developing the Realitychart, it is not always practical. In these instances, one-on-one formal interviews may be the best way to get information. While many sources provide information on how to conduct effective interviews, I have accumulated interviewing ideas from thousands of my students over the past twenty years. Some of these ideas will work for you, some may not. Use them accordingly.

The purpose of an interview is to gather causes and evidence of a historical event. Everyone will have a different perception, and people will nearly always tell the truth if given the chance. If they believe they will be punished or ridiculed, they may not participate or provide much value to your quest for information. Therefore, assume that everyone is telling their truth; to judge it otherwise during the interview would be a mistake on the interviewer's part.

Never find fault or place blame. The interview should be a well-planned and structured process focused on understanding what the interviewee perceives and should include feelings and evidence-based causes. Interviewing is about listening and empathizing. Listening includes observing nonverbal communication or body language. Many studies have shown that body language provides more than half of our communication, and those who fail to understand this will never be good interviewers.

Look for signs of frustration and ask the interviewee to tell you why they feel frustrated. Don't be afraid to divert from your initial line of questions if you see the opportunity to learn what is in the mind of the interviewee. Current brain studies show gut feelings are very real even though we are usually inadequate at explaining them.[1] Pursue these and other feelings as they relate to the event. Remember, the validity of any cause will be determined by the completion of the Realitychart, so do not attempt to make judgments during the interviewing process.

Prerequisites for Interviewing

The following are some prerequisites for interviewing:

1. The interviewee must have an incentive to participate. An incentive to participate can come from many quarters, but the need to be needed is perhaps the strongest need we humans have, and capitalizing on this is the interviewer's greatest tool. Putting yourself in the position of the student and the interviewee as the teacher will set the stage for an open dialog.

   Sometimes simply gaining approval or acceptance of their beliefs provides the incentive to participate.

   Occasionally people think they don't have anything to offer but have a need to learn what happened. If you think they know something and want to pursue it, their need to learn will provide an incentive. Share what you know and then ask them to fill in any blanks.

   There is no incentive if punishment is a consequence. Generally, interviewees are uncomfortable because they are fearful of punishment for themselves, others, or their group. If you have the authority to promise no punishment, then do so. Otherwise try to get them to see the greater value of learning from mistakes.

2. The interviewer must have credibility with the interviewee. If the interviewer doesn't have credibility, an alternative interviewer should be found. An antagonistic interview is worse than none at all because the negative feedback to the workforce will poison other information sources or future information gathering.

3. The interview must have a clear purpose. Be able to concisely state the purpose of the interview. If we do not understand why we are conducting an interview, it will be the first question the interviewee will ask. Based on my experience, interviews are often seen as a precursor to a hanging, so you need to have a clear understanding of the purpose. Fears can often be allayed by developing a Realitychart of the interviewee's reality because the interviewee sees where you are going with the questions. Be careful not to restrict yourself to the Realitychart unless you are well into the development of it and the purpose of the interview is to finish off a cause chain.

4. Understand the group dynamics prior to the interview. The politics of an organization can get you in trouble quicker than anything. For example, if the interviewee has a vendetta against his or her boss, the information may be very biased. If you do not know the politics or group dynamics of an organization going into an interview, try to find an unbiased person to help you.

5. Be prepared with predefined questions. A formal interview should never be an impromptu activity. Always spend time preparing questions so you have a direction. This does not mean you are restricted to these questions, but it provides initial structure. More often than not, your questions will not be used because the interviewee will take you to places you never dreamed of.

6. Be prepared to listen with an open mind. Listening is the key to effective interviewing. Suspending judgment or maintaining a positive bias while listening is just as important.

7. Dress appropriately. Unfortunately, we judge others by the first impression. One's appearance is an important part of setting the stage for success. Dress up or down depending on the situation. If you have to go to a dirty place, such as the location of the event, to conduct the interview, wear clothes that can get dirty, not formal or dressy attire.

8. Catch people at a relaxed time. If interviewees are busy performing their job or focused on work, they cannot be expected to have their minds on your questions. Creating a relaxed environment or finding such an environment to conduct the interview can reduce any worries they may have. Meal breaks may be a good time for interviews, although you need to be careful not to impose on someone's time or give the impression that the company won't take its time to investigate the problem.

9. Always meet on the interviewee's turf or at a neutral location. A neutral location is not the conference room next to the boss's office.

10. Sit on the same side of the table with the interviewee if possible. This will help create a relaxed environment, not one of interrogation. Also, it puts people "on the same side" in more than one way.

11. Schedule the interview. If you have an impatient interviewee, schedule the interview first and obtain approval from the supervisor if needed.

Starting the Interview

After an introduction and small talk to create a comfortable environment, explain the purpose of the interview and ask the interviewee if they are comfortable with sharing information. If not, then jump right into why they don't feel comfortable. Perhaps you have another problem or a cause somewhere in your current problem.

Communicate the common goal of preventing problem recurrence and meeting customer needs. Give the interviewee background on what you know about the event and what you hope to learn from this interview. Let interviewees know their names will not be used in any reports and make sure you follow through with this promise. There is no valid reason for including names in a report. Use titles or positions if necessary and be as general as you can be and still convey the message.

Start the questioning with open-ended questions. Open-ended questions are any questions that cannot be answered with a "yes" or "no." The best opening question is, "Please help me understand what happened?"

Avoid presenting yourself as a "know-it-all." Remember, you are the student and they are the experts. Don't be afraid to let them know you are fallible or don't know what is going on. If you did, you wouldn't be asking for their help. You must believe this to play it honestly.

Aspects of the Interview

Go slow at first. Let the interviewee "warm up." Keep on track with prepared questions, but encourage all relevant discussion. Use expressions such as "Go on. . .", "What does that mean to you?", or "Can you explain that further?" to continue a train of thought they may be struggling with. Sometimes it is appropriate to ask for feelings. "How did that make you feel?" can be a valid question if dealing with an emotional part of the event. Cause and effect is not limited to pure logic and reason. "Feeling Upset" is as valid a cause as "Leg Broken."

Always be honest in your dealings with others, but go out of your way to be this way in an interview. If you don't know something, say "I don't know." Sometimes the discussion leads to asking interviewees if they have any ideas how to find the answer. "I wonder who does know about that?" "Do you know anyone who might help us?" is a possible line of questions. Use follow-up questions to help focus the interview on a specific cause path, such as, "And that would mean. . .?" or "So what does that tell us about the causes?" "I don't understand; could you please elaborate?" is another good question to keep the thought process going. This helps build the interviewee's confidence that they are doing the right thing and are needed.

Maintain eye contact as much as possible to pick up on body language. If you are not skilled in reading body language, start learning or ask someone else to perform the interview. Eye contact is acceptable in most Western cultures but may be rude or even dangerous in some cultures.

Be enthusiastic about answers if the interviewee provides new insights. Do not be phony in this endeavor, but let interviewees know they are being helpful. Restate information by paraphrasing. This helps understanding. A good paraphrase should include a summary of the essential words (key nouns and verbs, not the modifiers), the emotional level from which the statements are made, and what value the interviewee places on them.

Avoid criticizing, complaining, or comparing and ask the interviewees to do the same if you catch them doing it. When responding to questions, use "I" not "we," "them," and "us" as this sets up a perception of different camps and can cause the interviewee to choose sides.

Take good notes or ask someone else to take notes while you do the interview. If you have a note taker, make sure you explain this function at the beginning of the interview.

Using "dead air" or an extended pause after a question often forces the interviewee to think more deeply about the question. We do not like dead air and hence feel a need to fill it with something. What may seem like a long time, often is not when things are quiet. This takes practice and doesn't always work, so use it according to your skills and the need to get the conversation going.

Closing the Interview

When the questions subside and there appears to be nothing more to learn, it is time to close the interview. A good question at the end of the interview is, "What would you do differently?" or "If you had a million dollars to spend on this problem, what would you do?"

Review your notes with the interviewee. If legible, show your notes to interviewees and ask them if they see anything you left out or that they want to add. The act of showing them your notes builds trust. You may even want to tell them you are going to do this at the beginning of the interview. Give a brief review of how helpful the interviewee has been (if true) and restate and write down any action items or commitments to get more information.

Explain what will be done with the information and promise to get back to them when the report is finished. Never pass up a chance to thank them and ask if there are any more questions before you leave. Ask if they can think of anyone else who might have information about this event or who could shed some light on the subject in general. Give interviewees your phone numbers and email address and ask them to contact you anytime they think of additional information. A good closing question is to ask if there was anything they expected you to ask that you didn't. Often people go into an interview with preconceived ideas and prepared answers. When you never get to their prepared answers, they may feel you didn't do your job but they may not speak up for fear of embarrassing you.

Dealing with Personnel Performance Issues

Interviewing someone who has been involved in less than stellar performance can often be very difficult for both the interviewee and the interviewer. While never easy, I have found that having internalized the cause-and-effect principle helps a great deal. By knowing that causes are infinite in nature and knowing that people do not purposefully attract negative attention by setting out to screw up, you can bust through the "I screwed up" barrier.

Starting with the effect of "screwed up" or "human error," ask why. As the individual who had the personnel performance problem reflects on the causes, they will focus on their actions. The person may say they pushed the wrong button, or said the wrong thing, or moved the wrong way. Each of these causes is an action cause, so try to identify the corresponding conditional causes that existed in the time before their action.

Remember that the cause-and-effect principle teaches us that every action has at least one conditional cause that existed in time before the action set the chain in motion to cause the undesirable effect. Finding these conditional causes often results in a big "aha" for everyone. More often than not, the individual has been set up to fail by the conditions of the task. When someone says, "I just screwed up," it should be a red flag for the interviewer. People do not come to work with the intent of making a mistake. Sure, some people do not pay attention or are incapable of learning, but it is incumbent on the facilitator to determine this with evidence-based causes, even if the individual believes he or she screwed up. This requires getting down to the causes between the causes and looking for human-based conditions.

If the action was "pushed the wrong button," you may want to determine what conditions were presented to the person. Was there enough light? Was the labeling correct? Was there adequate training and knowledge, etc.? The most difficult conditions to find and confront are the ones that lie within the human mind, such as "tired" or "confused."

I have found the following list provides a good source of ideas for questions to be asked when dealing with personnel performance issues:[2]

- *Too much information for the mind to comprehend*
- *Boring task*
- *Not proficient in task*
- *Unaware of action causes*
- *Lack of confidence*
- *Success in past experiences*
- *Weariness or fatigue*
- *Confusion*
- *Reactive response*
- *Memory lapse*
- *Fear of failure*
- *Priorities misaligned*
- *Spatially mis-oriented*
- *Inattention to detail*
- *Rigid mindset*
- *Myopic view of situation*
- *Scheduling pressure to complete task*
- *Lack of specific knowledge necessary to complete task*
- *Habit*
- *Inappropriate assumptions*
- *Used shortcuts*
- *Did not understand instructions*
- *Job performance standards not defined*
- *Disbelief in sensory input*
- *Used favorite indication instead of diverse input*
- *Indifferent attitude*
- *Righteousness or arrogance*
- *Inability to focus on task*

This list can be used to find possible cause paths for the lack of performance. For example, you may want to ask if the individual was fearful of failing or if they were sick or tired at the time of the action. If none of these apply or lead you to a clearer understanding of the causes, then perhaps it was inattentiveness or a failure to learn. Don't forget to continue asking why as you break through an emotional barrier with one of these possible causes.

A classic example of breaking through can be shown when pursuing the causes of an operator action. When asked why the operator made a mistake, the answer often comes back as "did not follow procedure." The investigation stops, and some favorite solution such as "rewrite the procedure" is offered and accepted. The problem here is stopping too soon. Break through this cause by continuing to ask why several more times until you get to "la-la-land" or the fuzzy zone. There are many reasons why people do not follow procedures and stopping at "did not follow procedure" will result in guaranteed recurrence.

Common Traps

Along the way to effective solutions, we encounter many traps. These are primarily ineffective human strategies that get in the way of the cause-and-effect principle. These traps are sometimes unique to the individual and sometimes apply to the team or group. In addition to the common causes of ineffective problem solving (such as storytelling, categorization, placing blame and the belief in common sense), the following is a list of common traps I have observed: consensus, groupthink, experts, parochial mindset, programmatic barrier, denial, and time as a cause.

All of these traps are discussed in some detail below so you can recognize them more readily. Guidance on how to deal with each one is also provided.

Consensus

The belief that the majority rules is so ingrained in our democratic belief system that consensus takes on the appearance of being a fundamental principle. While a very useful strategy, seeking consensus can be very detrimental. Most people are followers and want to be led. Tell them a good story they can connect with and they will follow along. The consensus trap follows this logic: "I am not really sure what is going on, but the collective knowledge of the group certainly could not be wrong, so I will go along."

The more people who follow, the more the consensus effect grows. Good leaders know this and capitalize on this herd mentality. While we use consensus to make decisions, we need to understand that consensus is an agreement to take a risk together, nothing more. If we want to minimize the risk, we need to base the decision to agree on evidence-based causal relationships, not innuendo and storytelling. An effective solution occurs because we understand the causal relationships, not because the consensus voted on it. Always use a Realitychart in your decision process.

Groupthink[3]

Groupthink is a term coined by the noted research psychologist Irving Janis (1918–1990) from Yale University and a professor emeritus at the University of California, Berkeley. He used the term to describe the systematic errors made by groups when making collective decisions. Groupthink is the condition of relinquishing our individuality for the perceived common good of the group. In fact, this perceived rightness by the group is a form of consensus that will doom the success of the group. Groupthink is subtle and the group may not recognize it unless they know what to look for. It is found in any group of people of any size working or playing together. It can be found in a married couple or an organized religion. It is a fundamental human condition and has proven very detrimental in our history.

The disaster at Pearl Harbor in 1941 was caused by the firm belief of Admiral Kimmel and his small staff that the Japanese would never attack them. The strength of this group belief, called groupthink, was unreasonable to a fault. Even when the bombs started falling, they thought it was a drill and couldn't understand who had authorized a drill on Sunday morning. Groupthink is characterized by many symptoms:

- *A belief that the group can do no wrong.*
- *A belief that the group has a higher authority than any individual inside or outside the group.*
- *Rationalization to justify a position established by the group, regardless of what other factors may be present.*
- *A strong sense of them and us.*
- *An atmosphere to conform. Anyone dissenting is ridiculed or put in a bad light to encourage conformity. Consensus holds the highest priority.*
- *Individual censorship based on the belief by individuals that they couldn't possibly be as smart as the entire group.*

- *The belief in group unity. Without ever calling for a vote, it is assumed that everyone in the group agrees to the same position. Sometimes this occurs even when the position goes unstated. The need for unity is so strong, potential conflicts are avoided or denied.*
- *Individuals speaking for the whole group.*

To prevent groupthink from getting started in your group or team, foster open discussion on any subject. Use a Realitychart to create a common reality based on evidence-based causes not storytelling or opinions of the strongest personality. Ask everyone to play devil's advocate and ask an outsider to review your work, if possible. Honestly address their comments. Avoid sharing conclusions outside the group discussion.

If you recognize the symptoms of groupthink as listed above, do the following:

1. Share what symptom you sense with the group. Let everyone know you think the group is falling into the trap of groupthink. If you get people who disagree strongly with your observations, then the group is probably engaging in groupthink.
2. Ask to be educated; play dumb with probing questions that bring a different perspective to the table.
3. Let team members know it is okay not to know, then work on developing a plan to find answers.
4. Use the Realitychart as the basis for your common reality. Remember to use evidence and always go to your point of ignorance and find out if someone outside the group can answer your questions.
5. Encourage outside points of view and take action to bring them into the group discussion.
6. Challenge all statements that are made by an individual speaking for the group, such as, "I think we can all agree."

Groupthink is a strong human trait and difficult to recognize because it feels so natural to belong to a winning team that we don't want to upset the appearance of successful decisions.

Experts

Experts are essential to effective problem solving, but they should not be given any more credibility than the next person with evidence-based causes. By definition, the expert is a narrowly focused person who knows a great deal about his or her subject matter, but they do not know everything. Experts have a tendency to be right-minded. If they present themselves as opinionated and having the correct solution, beware. Everyone has to play by the same rules when using the Realitychart. If the expert provides a cause, they must also provide evidence. If they have none, do not get into an argument, but put a question mark in the evidence box and move on.

As a young engineer I was taught to respond to clients' questions with the statement: "It is my engineering judgment that this is true." This seems like a rather shallow response to technical questions, but it worked. What amazed me was how readily the client accepted this, and how many engineers believe it to be an acceptable practice. The non-engineer has no comeback for such a statement and is left to accept it. It is not a question of whether the statement is valid, it is a question of making the statement without any evidence to support it. As a young engineer I didn't know any better, and it was common practice in my design engineering organization. I did not seek to defraud or mislead, rather to express an opinion and add some credibility to it with the rather baseless "engineering judgment" statement.

As I grew older and began to realize the misuse of this term not only in my profession but in all experts from laborer to physician, I stopped using it. Part of being human is wanting to speak authoritatively. If people let us get away with it, we use this strategy with great skill. When you encounter this strategy, avoid a contest of wills and the spewing of excrement from large barnyard animals and just ask for the evidence to put on your Realitychart. Often the opinion is based in fact, but the expert has not been challenged for so long they have forgotten. Ask for references, examples, or details of past experiences.

Parochial Mindset

Parochial mindset or provincial thinking is yet another human condition that limits effective problem solving. My travels throughout the world have convinced me that it exists everywhere. It is a significant barrier to effective solutions because it drives us right to our favorite solutions. It is the common belief within a group that if no one in the group knows the answer to a question, then there is no answer to be had anywhere.

The next time you are working on a problem with others, step back and watch the discourse. As the questions and answers unfold, eventually a question will go unanswered. That is, someone will ask a question and the air is still with silence. After a short pause, because we don't like dead air, someone will change the subject or ask a completely different question. At this point there occurs an unstated but conscious agreement by all players that there is no answer and any pursuit of one has no value. The cause chain is stopped and never followed up unless someone in the group understands and implements the rules of the RealityCharting process.

This is a most interesting observation to me because it is a totally irrational act on the part of very rational people. I have observed this in almost every group since I first discovered it. When asked why they stopped asking why, the team members acknowledge they stopped but seem perplexed that I am asking about it. They seem to believe it is obvious why they stopped. When I ask them if they think someone outside the group might have an answer, they will acknowledge the possibility but will not pursue it unless pushed.

Always go outside your group for answers to the unanswered why questions. It is incredibly arrogant to think that you or your group are the only ones on the planet who know what's going on. Even if you are working on a specialized problem within a specialized industry, there is usually someone else who may know about these causal relationships and be able to provide some insights. Go to your local university; they love to work on real-world events. Get on the Internet. Stopping too soon is a common reason for ineffective solutions.

Programmatic Barrier

Another cause of stopping too soon is the programmatic barrier. This is similar to the parochial mindset but has different origins. When following a cause chain, the programmatic barrier occurs as we reach a point where the answer to the next why question will result in questioning some organizational program. This seems to be caused by the fear of discussing an institutionalized program. To attack an established program will require much effort and probably not yield any changes, so we stop. Sometimes the solutions associated with the last cause are general. For example, we may find that someone stopped at "not adequately trained." Knowing that the training program is inviolate may cause the team to offer a solution of retraining without regard for the causes of ineffective training. To break through this barrier, always go to your collective point of ignorance on every cause path.

Denial

Denial is the strongest human attribute we have. Its roots are in groovenation, but it is manifested in many ways. The need to maintain our own reality is sometimes stronger than the need to learn new cause-and-effect relationships. Sometimes perceptions intrude upon our "realities" and cause major conflicts. I recently came across an example of this in the responses to a *National Geographic* article on lions feeding at night. One letter to the editor read as follows:

"I found the photographs very unsettling. They captured the victim animals at their most private and vulnerable moments—those of terror and death. I am outraged at your assumption that I want to see these struggles."

This person openly stated her wish to deny her perception because it conflicted with her "reality." Furthermore, she is "outraged" that someone else could see a different reality and want to share it.

A different reality was presented in another letter to the editor regarding the same story.

"My daughter, age four years nine months, looked over my shoulder as I was reading my August issue. She was so interested in the pictures of the lions that I had to read all the captions to her with minor deciphering of difficult words. She now understands that a night in the life of a lion is not exactly as it is for Simba in the movie *The Lion King*."

This parent not only enjoyed the sight of her reality, but shared it with her child.

While watching a television news magazine, I saw yet another incredible display of denial and how opinions become fact. The chief of public health for the state of Kentucky enlightened the viewers with this logic. "If tobacco sickness were real, we would know by now because we have been growing tobacco for over two hundred years." He said this with the full knowledge that hospitals and other medical facilities treat hundreds of people each year for tobacco sickness. Tobacco sickness is a common problem with people who work cutting and storing tobacco plants. The freshly cut tobacco secretes nicotine, a highly toxic alkaloid that is absorbed through the skin. It causes fainting, weakness, and sometimes death. But, according to some people, dying from tobacco sickness is not really a problem because it has been happening for over two hundred years.

When you observe someone denying what is in front of them, ask them to provide sensory evidence. Barring this, ask them to explain the causal relationships that support their views. This will usually help them overcome the misconception, but don't be surprised if they cannot offer an explanation. Denial is an incredibly strong aspect of the human condition.

Time as a Cause

Don't use time as a cause. Listen closely to our excuses. The cause is often given as time. We hear examples of this logic in daily conversation:

- *The reason my car looks so bad is because it is old.*
- *I couldn't finish my project because I ran out of time.*
- *I was late to work because time got away from me.*
- *We would have won the game if only there was more time.*

Things happen in time not because of time. The car does not look old because of time, nor is it worn out because of time. It is worn out because of use and the second law of thermodynamics—entropy, the natural law that dictates everything in the universe is trying to obtain it lowest energy state. There are many natural processes, such as friction and radiation that cause wear, and they happen in time not because of it.

Dealing with Group Interaction

As you go through the Square One Loop in a group setting, you will find four general types of interaction.

The Proverbial Storyteller

The storyteller will want to take you back to the scene of the problem and tell you all the people involved or give you a history lesson on why things are done the way they are. While this is often interesting and even informative, don't let them take control of the process. Listen carefully to what they are saying, and the first time you hear the answer to your why question, write it down, stop the story regardless of where it is, and ask why this cause happened.

Repeat this interruption process until you have mined all their causes. This will do more to shorten your meeting time than anything else you can do. Usually these storytellers begin to see what you are doing and realize that you only want causes and evidence. Because you are making progress and writing down what they have told you, they do not get upset with all the interruptions. Typically, they know you are trying to facilitate the process and will follow your lead, provided you are respectful and cordial. As you progress, they begin to see a better picture than the one that was in their own head.

The Analytic

The analytic is interested in why questions but is more interested in sharing the correct answer. Since they have typically analyzed the problem in great detail, their primary purpose is to make sure you understand the correctness of their ideas. More often than not, they have a very narrow perspective of the situation and have left out many other cause paths. They will even tell you why their perspective is the only possible one. Remind them of the infinite set of causes and interact with them just like you would the storyteller. Ask for a cause; as soon as you get it, interrupt them and ask why to that cause or that set of causes.

The analytics are more likely to become upset with you, so be patient with them. You don't want to turn off the information supply. The best method I have found to deal with this is to input every cause they give you. This validates their worth and they are more willing to let go. If they are really getting off track, ask them if you can let that cause path go for awhile and work on the other paths that may seem more productive.

Caution: If you are a storyteller or analytic, you should not be a facilitator unless you have had some facilitator training.

The Nonparticipant

The causes of nonparticipation can be numerous, but they often lie in the "don't know nothing" category or the "don't want to play this game" category. For those who honestly don't know anything about the problem, ask them for insights they may have after you have a good set of causes. The "dumb questions" are often the best. If they say they don't understand it, ask them to tell you why. If the Realitychart doesn't make sense, it is missing something. Use these people as your sounding board and honestly listen to them and make sure you understand why they don't see something. Also enlist their help in the solutions phase.

For the person who does not want to play, the cause could be fear of embarrassment or fear of implicating themselves or others. In either case, let them know there is no wrong answer. They can say anything that makes sense to them and if it fits into the Realitychart, it will be incorporated. For those fearful of being blamed, let them know that the purpose of this process is to find a solution that prevents recurrence, not to place blame or punish. Be careful not to give the assurance of no punishment unless you have that authority. Sometimes managers will usurp the investigator and your credibility is forever destroyed. This is often a tight balancing act because in about 1% of the situations, punishment may be the best solution. Try to identify the possibility of punishment before getting into the details of problem analysis. If it is possible, do not grant amnesty in these cases but continue to develop the Realitychart.

The Participant

The participant is eager to learn and understand what happened. This eagerness is sometimes slow in coming because of painful experiences in previous group problem solving, but it will come in time. The true participant is usually quick to pick up on the basic rules of this process and the importance of causes and evidence. They begin to realize that the facilitator is more interested in why, and that the who question is never asked. With a consistently honest approach in asking why, the participants gain confidence and open up as more causes are understood. When someone knows the answer to a sincerely asked question, it is hard for them not to share what they know. It is especially hard if they can see how much clearer the picture will be when they add their knowledge to the common reality being created. People fundamentally want to help others, but they must be assured they will not suffer the pain of embarrassment. This can be accomplished by letting everyone know there is no such thing as a right or wrong answer in this process; there are only causes and evidence.

Facilitation Guidelines: Some Q&A

The following guidelines respond to commonly asked questions. They are intended to provide a quick reference if you get into trouble while facilitating or if you want a quick review before starting.

How do I maintain meeting focus?

Stay in the Square One Loop; focus on why and how you know (evidence). Minimize storytelling and over-analysis by forcing the team to focus on causes. Explain the process to newcomers if needed.

How do I handle team outliers?

For those who already have the right answer, ask them to let the process work for awhile. Remind them that you will get to the solutions only after you know all the causes. If this doesn't work, ask them how they know their answer is the best one. As they explain, listen for causes not yet shown and add them to the Realitychart. Often we know a good solution but don't know why. Our unconscious mind has already figured it out. We call this "gut feel" and it can be very effective if we understand the causal relationships behind it. Once we know the causal relationships, others can appreciate it and be assured that the gut-feel answer is based in causes.

For the defensive person, let them know the purpose of this process is to fix the problem, not to place the blame. Be very careful here; if you do not have the authority to grant amnesty, don't offer it. Never ask, "Who did this?"

For the boisterous or assertive person, ask them to hold their comments, and remind them you are looking for causes and evidence, not stories. Explain the difference if needed.

Remember, the need to be needed is the strongest human need; use it to your advantage, such as with the shy person. "Please help me to understand what happened here."

For excuse givers, ask them to define the problem as they see it. Listen carefully and write down the causes they give you. Insert the causes into the Realitychart and then ask for evidence. If the excuse givers have no evidence, put a question mark under the cause and move on.

How do I stimulate discussion?

Everyone has an opinion—ask for it.

Everyone needs to be needed. Ask people to help you figure this out using questions such as, "Please help me to understand what happened."

Be dumb like a fox; ask simple, probing questions.

Use provocation; make an absurd statement or challenge conventional wisdom.

Use small talk to get people relaxed, then ask for feelings or perceptions.

How do I prevent manipulation of the RealityCharting process ?

If someone on the team is trying to manipulate the causes to exclusively show their reality, make sure you follow the first three steps of the RealityCharting process without exception. This is often obvious because the chart stops too soon and has few branches.

To force a broader perspective, look for actions and conditions at every node.

Always demand evidence.

Challenge the obvious and conventional wisdom—it is often biased and incomplete.

Challenge or test the belief that the solution will prevent recurrence.

Go outside the group for a separate review.

Be on the alert for groupthink.

How do I avoid embarrassing the participants?

Follow the fundamental rules of chart development.
Establish an open learning environment from the very beginning.
Never ask, "Who did it?"
Avoid any judgmental statements.
Write down every stated cause.
Let the team members know that in the RealityCharting process, there is no such thing as right and wrong, only causes and evidence.

Is evidence that critical?

Evidence is one of the most important elements of the RealityCharting process. If you fail to use it, you may be setting yourself up to fail. Having said that, it is less important than getting all perspectives to fit on the chart.
Try to find sensory evidence and if you do not have it, use inferred evidence. Try to identify two or more ways to document evidence.

How do I ensure precise cause statements?

Use noun-verb statements.
Try to limit the number of words to four or fewer.
Avoid prepositions in the cause statement if you can. This includes terms such as "of," "to," "before," "but," and "against."

How do I write clear corrective actions?

Always use specific corrective actions. Identify the individual(s) responsible for implementing the actions and specify the completion date.
Avoid using "re-" words, such as "retrain."
Never use study or analyze; if you do, you are not done.
If you cannot connect a solution to one of the causes on the Realitychart, either your solution or your chart is incomplete.

How can I use cause categorization?

Cause categorization should be avoided except as guidance when you cannot get any answers to the why questions. Look for causes in people, procedures, hardware, and the environment by asking what role each category played. This will lead you to more specific why-type questions.

What are the qualities of a good finished product?

Assiduous adherence to the first three steps of the RealityCharting process will ensure an effective solution. The essential elements of a good report include (a) a well-defined problem statement, (b) a complete

Realitychart with evidence, and (c) solutions that attack one or more causes on the chart while meeting the four solution criteria.

What do I do if no causes come?

Look for causes in actions and conditions.
Look for causes in categories.
Look for differences and when you find them, ask why.
Use other problem-solving tools, but always come back to the Realitychart.

How do I resolve a stalemate discussion?

If you have a group of headstrong people who do not value appreciative understanding, ask one team member to create a strawman Realitychart based on how they see the problem. When completed, this strawman chart will be used by all team members to criticize and tear apart, so don't give this task to a right-minded egotist, who knows the right answer. Since it is always easier to criticize than create, the strawman Realitychart moves the group from a creative consensus mode, which is not working, to a completely critical mode, which is building a new common reality.

How do I overcome storytelling?

Use the Square One Loop.
Let the storyteller go until you hear some causes. As you hear the causes, write them down. As long as causes are coming from the story, let it continue; but if the story digresses to discussion of people, places, and things as a function of time, stop it. Put the causes on a Realitychart and ask the team to help you put them in order using why and "caused by." When you get all of the causes placed, pick one at the end of a chain, and ask the storyteller, "Why this cause?" Continue this process until you run out of causes.

Is fostering goodwill worth it?

Fostering goodwill may seem like an extra step not worth taking, but problem solving is a continuous part of doing business and anything to promote goodwill is worthwhile. Always send a copy of the final report to everyone who helped in the problem-solving process and thank them for their help. Give special thanks for extraordinary help. Celebrate all major successes by letting everyone know the value added by the solutions. If you had a problem that had occurred ten times over the past five years and it cost $10,000 for each failure, calculate the savings that the solution is going to create and publish it to the broadest audience you can.

Facilitating Groups

The RealityCharting problem-solving process is most effective when used in a group. Facilitating a group to find effective solutions can be challenging, but it is very rewarding when you arrive at corrective actions without conflict and argument.

The best advice I can give for anyone engaged in group facilitation of the RealityCharting process is to have faith in the process. It will work if you just follow the first three steps: define the problem, create a Realitychart, and identify effective solutions. Within each success, we always have small failures, such as someone who doesn't want to participate or the proverbial storyteller who won't quit talking, but if you are reflective, you will learn from each incident and get better with time.

With each new incident, you will be presented with the vast collection of human perspectives. Wisdom will lead you to better understand the notion that there is no such thing as one right answer, but because there is an infinite set of causes, you can always find an effective solution.

References

1. Rita Carter. *Mapping the Mind*. Los Angeles: University of California Press (1999).
2. *Human Performance Enhancement System Coordinator Manual*, INPO 86-016 (Rev. 3), Atlanta, Georgia: (1986).
3. Irving L. Janis. *Groupthink: Psychological Studies of Policy Decisions and Fiascoes*.

13
Success and Serendipity

Those who have succeeded at anything and don't mention luck are kidding themselves.

—Larry King

Now that we have a better understanding of the principles of causation and how they can be used to help us understand how our world works, let's take a closer look at how causal thinking can help us be more successful at our endeavors. We will explore different strategies for success and examine how luck or chance fits into the causal structure of reality.

Serendipity, accident, happenstance, chance, luck, and probability are all players in the world of cause and effect, but what are they? How do they present themselves in the structural framework of cause and effect—or are they causes unto themselves? This is a question that has lingered in the back of my mind for years because they are such a dominant part of the causal world. Without happenstance and variability, I would not be writing this book nor would I have explored the world of causation because everything would already be determined.

Before we get into the structure of these qualities, we need to understand what they are, or at least how we use these words to help us understand our world.

Serendipity Defined

"Serendipity" is a word coined by Horace Walpole (1754) taken from a fairy tale "The Three Princes of Serendip." As the story goes, the three princes were always making pleasant discoveries by chance and keen perception. (Note: Serendip is currently known as Sri Lanka.) Perhaps one of the most famous modern examples of serendipity was the discovery of Post-It® Notes where a researcher for 3M found a use for a failed glue he had created.

The microwave oven was invented by Percy Spencer while testing a magnetron for radar sets at Raytheon. During the test, he noticed that a candy bar in his pocket had melted while he was standing in front of the magnetron transmitter.

If we look at this event causally, we see two systems. The candy bar system in Figure 13.1 and the microwave system in Figure 13.2.

These two systems existed in and of themselves, totally separate from one another and they had never before come together that anyone knew about until the fateful day that Percy Spencer came to work with a candy bar in his pocket. At that time the two systems occupied the same space and time, thus satisfying the fourth principle of causation. Occupying the same space was caused by Percy's action of stepping in front of the magnetron transmitter while it was operating. So three causes, each from a different system, came together for the first time. Specifically, the conditional cause of "Candy Bar In Pocket" came together with the conditional cause of "Microwave Signal In Air" by virtue of the action cause by Percy stepping in front of the magnetron. But serendipity requires other actions, such as the intelligence to ask why, the knowledge

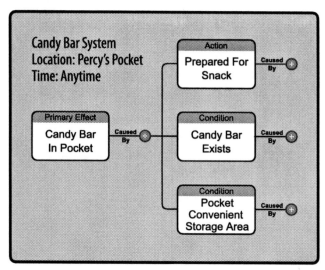

Figure 13.1. Candy Bar System

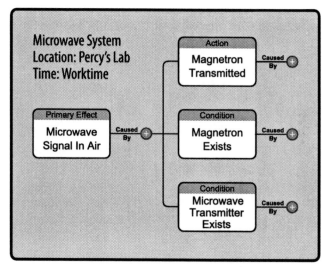

Figure 13.2. Microwave System

to find the answers, and the tenacity to do something with the newfound knowledge. All these causes are shown in Figure 13.3 and help us better understand the structure of serendipity.

While "serendipity" is used to describe a positive happenstance coupled with intelligence, the word "accident" is often used to describe a negative happenstance and is often coupled with ignorance or failure to think causally.

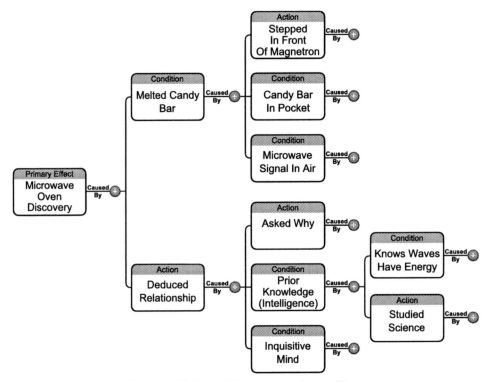

Figure 13.3. Microwave Oven Discovery

In the example shown in Figure 13.4, we see that the hypothetical drowning "accident" was caused by the "Person" system coming together with the "River" system by virtue of the action cause "Fell Out Of Boat." And, instead of other conditional causes, such as intelligence and thinking causally, this event contains the causes of ignorance and poor choices.

Be it serendipity, chance, or an accident, we can see from these examples the basic structure of how "stuff happens." Our world is made of many systems, all doing their own thing and eventually interacting with another system to cause a new event or a new system. And the more we learn and grow our knowledge, the more new systems there are to interact, so the world gets ever more complicated and more "stuff happens."

"Happenstance" is the circumstance of "chance," where "chance" and "luck" are qualities shared by unexpected, random, or unpredictable events. The key words here being "shared events," as we saw in the examples above.

By understanding that happenstance can be caused by the coming together of two or more systems, we can purposefully bring different systems together and observe the effects, called an "experiment," or we

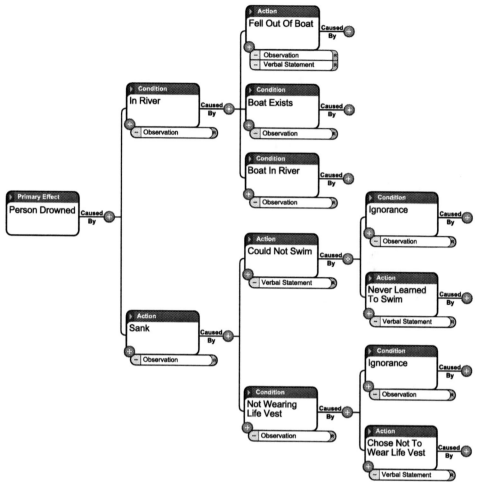

Figure 13.4.   Person Drowned

can make sure certain systems do not share any causes as a way of ensuring a safe and desired outcome. Wearing a life vest or learning to swim would alter the human system to prevent the undesirable effect of drowning.

Furthermore, with this understanding we can see that by bringing unrelated and previously unconnected systems together, we are setting the stage for serendipity—for a chance to discover something new. We just have to be more like the princes of Serendip and use our intuition and intelligence to discover the positive effects that may occur.

Understanding the structure of chance allows us to adopt a learning strategy of bringing different systems together and being very observant of the resulting causal relationships. Simply subjecting oneself to new experiences can facilitate serendipity. The more we know about the causes of the systems around us, the more likely we are to discover something new—to experience serendipity.

And what about "probability," aren't all these qualities just a matter of probability which can be statistically determined given enough data? We know that systems will come together, it is just a matter of when, so isn't this just probability? Probability is an educated guess about the likelihood of a given event to occur, but this says nothing about the structure of happenstance. To learn more about probability and statistics, go to http://coach.RealityCharting.com/book/probability.

To help us further understand chance, let's go back to the basics and look at the elemental causal set where we see that for every effect we have at least one condition and one action. The conditions of every event are just sitting there in their own space and time waiting for an action to come along and cause an effect. The available actions exist as part of any system, so not only do we find interaction between systems, we can have variability within a given system caused by changing conditions and actions. For example, we could define a system for every living creature on the planet and it could be unique for that creature because each one has the ability to respond to its own environment and that response is not always predetermined. In lower life forms, a specific stimulus is more likely to result in the same response, but even here mutations or deviations from the norm exist. In higher life forms, like humans, the uniqueness of every mind presents an infinite set of possible responses for a given stimulus. So, in all human systems or systems that include human actions, the chance of an effect occurring is caused by the infinite variability of human actions in the presence of given conditions at a certain point in time and space. So, "stuff happens," and we call it "chance" or "coincidence" or "accident," etc.

Knowing that this variability in human systems exists helps us understand that when we set about providing solutions to a problem, it is best to apply our solutions to conditional causes rather than action causes. This is particularly true if the action involves a human because the next time the system encounters the same set of causes there may be a different human and thus a different effect.

Knowing the structure of happenstance and the infinite set of causes that represents reality also helps us understand the unexplained. The human condition often demands answers even where there are none, and because of this seemingly natural condition, we create answers in direct violation of the principles of causation and the reality of happenstance. With this new understanding we can demystify the many unhealthy human belief systems that rely on mystery and intrigue to sell certainty about the unknown. By seeing the world as many systems operating in their own space and time, each with its own set of infinitely variable action causes, we can recognize that the unknown is knowable, or if it is not currently knowable, we can accept the unknown as only a temporary condition in the infinite set of causes that is reality. Instead of creating a belief system dependent on certainty or "Truth", we can dedicate ourselves to continuous learning and free ourselves from the contradictions that always arise from a belief in certainty. Some things may be unknowable, but the more we realize we live in a universe of cause and effect, the more we can approach with confidence every current unknown as a temporary condition. To do otherwise squanders our birthright as conscious, thinking human beings.

How to Have a Nice Day

When we set out each morning to interact with the world, we are hopeful that we will have a good day. Achieving that goal depends on two things, serendipity and the conditions in which we find ourselves throughout the day. Since serendipity is by definition beyond our control, our happiness is often left to our ability to control the conditions around us—to include those that foster serendipity or prevent accidents. Controlling these conditions is a form of problem solving, so the better our problem-solving skills, the greater the chance for a good day and a good life.

People who have a good day are not necessarily lucky, wealthy, or smart. Perhaps the key to any human success, no matter how you define it, is to control the infrastructure in which you live such that it assures the best outcome when chance or serendipity enters your life. Since everything that happens is caused to happen, the better we can understand the causes around us, the better we will be at controlling them to a satisfactory end.

By controlling or establishing the conditions of a particular situation, we can anticipate random and unwanted actions such that the outcome or effect is beneficial or at least not harmful. For example, the condition of having a college education will provide opportunities to control more causes resulting in more income and thus more nice days. Or, the fact that I am here writing this book today is partially caused by my understanding that some people are irresponsible and talk on their cell phones while driving, which causes inattention, and which recently caused a driver to run a stop light at over fifty miles per hour at an intersection where I was waiting for the green light. And because I was watching for her to stop before I entered the intersection and saw that she was not going to, I did not enter the intersection as the green light allowed me to and certainly would have resulted in a horrific T-bone crash and possible death for me. I had a nice day, but it could have been a very bad one had I not understood the world causally and relied, instead, on others to follow the rules or for chance or destiny to takes its course.

By understanding this simple concept at a philosophical level, it empowers us to fight a common set of practices that causes a dedication to ignorance so prevalent in the human condition. Stuff does not just happen and there is no such thing as magic, only cause and effect and the unknown. To be more successful than the next person, learn to ask why until you reach your point of ignorance and then find someone who can answer what you don't know until you have a clear, causal understanding of the event in question. The more events you understand at a causal level, the more you will be able to predict, and thus affect, the outcome at the beginning of the event and thus the more good days you will have. Think causally and have a nice day.

Cultural Strategies

The human mind is designed to recognize patterns and sequences in time such that when we see the first part of a pattern developing, we will be able to predict the rest of the pattern and know what conditions will affect a favorable end condition. This pattern recognition is an inherent part of all problem solving by most living creatures.[1] We learn that if the hungry stomach is to be quieted, we must fill it. To fill it, we must acquire food, to acquire food, we must buy it or grow it and then prepare it properly. To buy food, we need money; to get money we must work. To have a job, we must have knowledge and skill—the more knowledge and skill, the better our lifestyle, etc. There is an infinite number of combinations of causes by which we choose to accomplish this simple and common goal of satisfying a basic need and we call this a *strategy*. We each use many strategies to accomplish the various goals we set for ourselves and our communities. Perhaps the most important and earliest of all human strategies is that of cooperation and respect for others. In our short sixty-thousand-year existence, every human culture that violated this strategy of cooperation and respect ultimately failed and no longer exists.[2]

Our end goal is always survival and there is an infinite number of human strategies used to accomplish this goal.[3] Since the dawn of humanity, we gathered in communities because we understood the value of working together to accomplish common goals. In each community, we assembled a set of strategies, which became the culture for that community.

By our very nature, humans have always experimented with things in our environment to better understand causal relationships and to learn how we can control them to our advantage. Fire makes us warm and it can cook our food, and it fights off predators or it can melt rocks into metal that allow us to make tools, and it can help send us to the moon—and the learning goes on. There is no end to our quest for knowledge, but almost every culture in human history eventually became complacent, arrogant, and righteous in their belief that they hold the key to human happiness. Historically, when the happiness did not come for everyone in the community, some people left these communities to form new ones with new strategies and thus new cultures.[2] With each new culture came conflict with the older cultures because the new strategies contradicted the elders' truths. The struggle of cultures has never stopped and continues today as a natural part of the greater human culture. Whether new or old, every successful culture has some common strategies, while those cultures that have failed or are currently failing are doing so because of failed strategies.

Successful cultural strategies include:

> Cooperation; working together for a common goal.
> Dedication to learning; openness to change.
> Everything is caused to happen; no mysteries.
> Freedom from tyranny; democracy.

Let's look a little closer at each one of these strategies to see what we can learn.

Cooperation and Respect

While we all hold different perspectives of the world, the one strategy that allows us to coexist with others is cooperation coupled with the respect for other beliefs. Anthropologists believe that this one strategy is perhaps a critical cause of what we know as the human species today.[2] Without this strategy, cooperation in controlling our environment is nearly impossible. Without the tinker, the tailor, and the candlestick maker or the carpenter, the farmer, and the baker, a viable existence is not possible in a harsh land. One of the most interesting examples of this strategy extends beyond the human-to-human relationship to that of our relationships with dogs—man's best friend. Every breed of dog has 99.8% wolf genes. In the remaining 0.2% there are some genes that control the amount of testosterone the animal will produce which in turn causes domestication. The lower the testosterone, the gentler the animal—dog or human. Dogs are domestic and gentle because they have been genetically bred to be so. Ten to twenty thousand years ago, ancient man created dog by only allowing the most gentle of wolves to stay around the camp. Even more interesting is that with the domestication genes come different physical characteristics such as size, shape, fur pattern, and color. Once these new characteristics presented themselves, humankind bred for the characteristics they wanted in the dog. Proof that mutual respect naturally provides major benefits for both parties is that the wolf is on the edge of extinction and dogs are growing more popular every day. Not only did the dog or what was formerly the wolf follow a successful causal path to survival, humanity benefited from this relationship as well. There are also many examples in human history where dogs have played a critical role in the survival of humans such as the sled dogs of the north or dogs that helped people hunt game to survive.

Be it man or beast, mutual respect and cooperation have proven to be effective strategies for millennia.

Dedication to Learning

If the culture does not include learning new things and holds strictly to the past, it is only a matter of time before it and the people who live within that culture disappear. You do not have to look far into human history to see this consequence. Aboriginal people on all continents have disappeared or are fading away today. Every culture that has focused on learning has been more successful than the ones that do not, but this is also limited by what is learned. If the culture uses the strategy that what is already known is all you need to know, to include ritualistic dogma, and it does not allow the individual freedom to learn new things, then the culture will stagnate and eventually be left behind and die—it is only a matter of time. If you think about this for a moment, you can see this struggle going on today between the ancient cultures of the world and the more successful modern cultures that have a strong dedication to science, technology, engineering, and mathematics. As the young people of these ancient cultures examine the reasons why they are being left behind (with impoverished citizens) and see other cultures in the world growing more affluent, these ancient cultures know they will have to change.

Causal Thinking

Since everything that happens is caused to happen, one of our most important strategies is understanding causal relationships. While our brains are very good at recognizing causal relationships, anything beyond about three causal connections becomes too complex for most minds to handle at one time, so we have learned to utilize various tools to help us understand complex things. While humans have created many tools, such as mathematics, language, and the laws of the physical sciences, we have historically struggled with understanding complex causal relationships. By understanding the cause-and-effect principle and the RealityCharting process which is derived from these principles, it is now possible to overcome one of our greatest barriers to understanding complex systems.

Freedom of Thought

Freedom from tyranny is a basic human need and humanity has been fighting against tyranny since our beginning. It is only in recent history that a few cultures have been able to overcome the tyrants and many more are following precedent because their survival is at stake and they know it. There is a clear causal connection between freedom and world peace. Freedom from tyranny means that individuals have the freedom to seek their own version of happiness without the dogma of others. And, so long as this path to happiness does not infringe on other's rights to the same thing and so long as respect is maintained, prosperity always follows. With prosperity comes more freedom and happiness and we are less likely to engage in cultural conflicts (wars). As you look around the world and identify those pockets of human freedom, you observe prosperity and the resultant peace. When you observe those places of tyranny and dedication to the past, you often see rampant poverty, turmoil, and strife. This is not because of chance, but because the cultures do not include effective principle-based strategies, to include personal freedom of thought and the expression thereof.

Effective Personal Success

The strategies above are mostly part of a group culture; the following personal strategies can help make life's journey a more pleasant one.

Principle-based Strategy

In his landmark book , *The Seven Habits of Highly Effective People,* Stephen Covey provides a very effective formula for success. At the core of his teachings is the notion of a principle-centered strategy, which requires that all your strategies be principle-based. Because principles work the same way for everyone every time, like a compass, they can be trusted to help you meet your goals, but they are not always easy. Humans tend to seek the path of least resistance and want to push the "Easy" button to attain their goals, while principles, hard or easy, can provide the best path to success because they work every time.

However, because human behavior is not easily changed, especially when a behavior is hard wired in the brain, like categorization, taking the harder path that is principle based is not always the most successful path because humans easily fall off the path and resort to old habits. It's harder to learn new things than it is to follow the path of ignorance and educational stasis. In his book *The Path of Least Resistance for Managers*, Robert Fritz, elegantly explains that because the underlying structure of anything will determine its path of least resistance, to change behavior, we may need to change the underlying structure of the path so that it is the easiest path.[4] This is what RealityCharting® does—it makes the path to effective solutions easier than ever before and unlike the other problem solving methods, it is principle based.

Prioritizing

As we go through life trying to figure out how to accomplish our goals we are presented with endless options. As our world continues to get ever more complicated, choosing where to expend one's energy can be a daunting task. By understanding the causal relationships of all the systems we interact with we are better able to know which causes to apply solutions to, solutions that provide the best return on our invested time. When presented with several tasks and limited time, evaluate each task to determine which one will provide the best return for the time invested and then focus on that task. The evaluation can be as simple as listing the pros and cons of each goal or you can use more complex decision making processes. For a detailed discussion of different prioritizing schemes, go to http://coach.RealityCharting.com/book/decisionguide. This is a document developed for the US Department of Energy in 2001, titled Guidebook to Decision Making Methods.

Focus

Once we have prioritized which tasks to work on, we must not deviate from the task at hand. In today's world there is much emphasis on multitasking, but tests have shown that the brain simply cannot effectively multitask. When tested, those who think they are good at multitasking show less than stellar outcomes of the tasks at hand. According to Earl K. Miller who is a neuroscience professor at MIT, "People can't multitask very well, and when people say they can, they're deluding themselves," and he added, "The brain is very good at deluding itself." Miller, goes on to state that for the most part, we simply can't focus on more than one thing at a time. What we can do, he said, is shift our focus from one thing to the next with astonishing speed. "Switching from task to task, you think you're actually paying attention to everything around you at the same time. But you're actually not," Miller said. "You're not paying attention to one or two things simultaneously, but switching between them very rapidly."

Most successful people have the ability to focus and stay focused on a given task. Controlling our attention allows us to ignore the random stimulus that imprisons many people and this control is a core characteristic of most successful entrepreneurs. Being able to effectively focus allows one to develop principle-based strategies and have better self-control, which help cause more success in life. Security is not caused by a good job or money, but in your ability to interact with your environment better than the next fellow, to accomplish your goals. And this is caused by the ability to stay focused long enough to figure out the causal relationships of surrounding events.

Positive Attitude

Perhaps one of the most important strategies is to stay positive about life and what you can accomplish. Having a positive attitude will not cause you to be happy in and of itself—rather it is just one of many causes and it will help overcome some of the frustrations in life, so you can stay focused on more important issues. It has recently been shown that optimism is a genetic trait and most humans have it[5], so buck up and be happy.

Continuous Improvement

As discussed earlier, the more we know, the more we know we don't know, so success requires learning. This is more easily understood by looking once again at the cause-and-effect principle, which states that every effect must have at least two causes. As we progress down every causal path, we will eventually come to our point of ignorance where we no longer have answers but, because we know that there are at least two answers to the last why question, there is much more to know. Figure 13.5 shows this relationship and helps us understand the fundamental

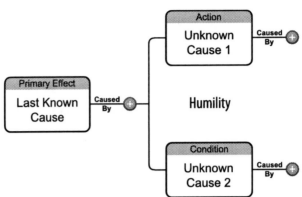

Figure 13.5. Humility Defined

reason why we should abandon our arrogant attitudes of certainty in anything we think we know and be humble in everything we know. By understanding that we need to be humble in our beliefs, we know that we can always learn more by questioning conventional wisdom and seeking to learn as much as we can about important subjects. Unfortunately, the human condition is dedicated to seeking the path of least resistance, which causes intellectual laziness resulting in complacency, ignorance, and arrogance. To avoid this trap, adopt a strategy of learning. It can be fun because it stimulates the mind. The brain doesn't care what causes the dopamine rush that causes happiness, so we have a choice to stimulate the brain with learning or playing mindless games. If you want to be a winner at life rather than the winner of a mindless game, choose to stimulate your mind with knowledge and leave the mindless games to others.

Tenacity

"If at first you don't succeed, try, try again," goes the old adage. By knowing that every effect is part of an infinite continuum of causes, we can see that success and failure are both caused to happen; the difference being that success is planned and failure is not. The better we can understand the causes of success, the better we can plan for it. RealityCharting can be used to show the causes of success or the causes of failure; they are both defined and best understood by knowing the causal relationships. If a failure occurs and then we fail to adequately understand and learn from the failure, it is a double failure. Understanding the causal relationships of an event can be a lot of work and takes discipline—regardless, stay focused and keep asking why.

Humility Meets Arrogance

As we just learned, the more we know, the more we know we don't know. To think otherwise is incredibly arrogant, yet it is a fundamental characteristic of the human condition. In our short human history, more humans have suffered a premature death by tenaciously holding to false ideas than by any other cause.

But arrogance can also be a good thing if it is directed toward learning. For example, it is incredibly arrogant to think we can fly, but we can with the aid of an airplane, which was developed by principle-based, highly focused, tenacious people seeking improved conditions, using a causal understanding of the world in a positive fashion. Those who ignore these strategies and believe in some tyrannical certainty are doomed to follow a path of mediocrity or outright failure depending on the happenstance of their times.

References

1. Rita Carter. *Mapping The Mind*. Los Angeles: University of California Press (1999).
2. Spencer Wells. *The Journey of Man*. Princeton, NJ: Princeton University Press (2002).
3. Daniel Goleman. *Emotional Intelligence*. New York: Bantam Books (1995).
4. Robert Fritz, *The Path of Least Resistance*, San Francisco, Berrett-Koehler Publishers (1999)
5. http://genome.wellcome.ac.uk/doc_WTX053787.html.

14

A New Way of Thinking

A mind once expanded never regains the same shape.

—Adapted from Oliver Wendell Holmes

Event-based problem solving is quite simple once we understand the structure of causation. It is my hope that with RealityCharting®, RealityCharting Simplified™, and RealityCharting Coach more people will begin to appreciate how much more effective they can be at event-based problem solving, both in their business lives and personal lives. The RealityCharting process has the following attributes.

- *Can be used by everyone*
- *Offers a structured approach*
- *Applies to all event-based problems*
- *Does not require checklists or forms*
- *Minimizes storytelling*
- *Creates a common reality*
- *Encourages a questioning attitude*
- *Provides a platform for creative solutions*

Effective solutions for everyday problems are guaranteed every time if you choose to implement these tools.

When it comes to event-based problems, effective problem solving has long eluded us. It doesn't matter what industry, what company, or what country, based on my studies, the average problem-solving effectiveness for most organizations is about 30%. Repeat events are so common we develop trending programs to measure them and we fail to see the contradiction this presents.

RealityCharting Process

The RealityCharting process is effective because it is principle-based and works naturally with all points of view. It works in conjunction with all perspectives to allow a common reality to emerge from the diversity of each stakeholder. As we have seen, the methodology is simple in structure and form. It can be used by anyone on all event-based problems without the use of checklists or forms. It counteracts the ineffective human strategies of storytelling and categorization by creating an evidence-based common reality of cause-and-effect relationships. By appreciatively understanding all perspectives, the methodology encourages a questioning attitude and serves as a platform for creative solutions anchored in fact, not politics, fantasy, or delusion.

By providing structure and form to problem solving, we can begin to teach problem solving as a subject unto itself. By breaking out of the old paradigm that problem solving is inherent to the subject matter, we can begin to teach people how to think and communicate in a way that provides effective solutions to event-based problems every time. Simply by knowing that there is an infinite set of causes and that every effect has at least two causes we can break out of the linear thinking that has prevented effective problem solving since the beginning of human history.

The RealityCharting process is to effective solutions what mathematics is to accounting and engineering. Before we had numbers, humans had very limited accomplishments. Without numbers we could not measure nor engage in serious trade. But a formal numbering system did not happen overnight. Ascribed to Pythagoras, mathematics was not considered a subject of serious study until about 500 B.C., and it wasn't until the Renaissance of the seventeenth century that mathematics fully blossomed and eventually led us to the Industrial Revolution.

Like the evolution of mathematics, the struggle to find a better way to communicate is slow to develop. We have not developed a set of rules by which to effectively and consistently solve event-based problems—until now. By recognizing the disparity between our linear language and the nonlinear physical world we live in, we see the elegance of the Realitychart. We finally have a tool that allows all stakeholders to visualize and share the causes of any event-based problem.

Our linear thinking has misguided us into the narrow-minded thinking of a root cause for every problem. This thinking is born of our language, or perhaps it is the language that shapes our thinking. Either way, when we limit ourselves to think only in terms of A caused B and B caused C, we limit our ability to address the complex issues we must face in our rapidly changing world. This is not to say we should stop telling stories and forget about simple linear cause chains. This is not going to happen and it should not happen. Telling stories is one of the greatest things about being human, and short cause chains often occur in the cause-and-effect charts, but we should leave stories to the world of entertainment and adopt causal thinking for all matter associated with event-based problems and our success for the future.

Expressing branched cause paths like those presented herein is too difficult for our modern languages. By producing a Realitychart, we are providing a visual dialog that enables all stakeholders to learn together such that they arrive at a common solution.

People walk away from a RealityCharting session with the gratification that their perspective was included and that the causes make sense. Everyone is confident the solution will work because they can see the causal connections between solution and primary effect. Intuition and gut feelings are even represented if the group concurs with the value. There is a realization that while they did not arrive at their original conclusion, things have to be done differently.

If someone did not participate in the original construction of the chart, it facilitates future visual dialog to accommodate new perspectives. This learning process is enabled by the visual dialog and is a better motivator for improvement than implementing what somebody else dictates.

A Simple Structured Approach

As with a wheel or anything of great value, it is the simplicity that provides the greatest worth. We can take the man out of the cave, but it has been virtually impossible to take the cave out of the man. While we humans have come a long way toward improving our lifestyles, we still have the same brains we had when we lived in caves. We are very simple-minded creatures living in a very complex world, and by working together we have accomplished things no individual could ever hope to do.

When we come together to accomplish things as a group, we tap the power of the team, but not without some difficulty. As we learned from this adventure, as much as we would like to think we are created the same and want to be the same, we are as diverse and unique as each snowflake that falls. Finding a way to overcome the discord this causes and the problem of a linear language in a nonlinear world, while accommodating the simple human mind, has been a challenge for the ages. I believe this challenge has been met with the RealityCharting process. While the RealityCharting process is highly effective, it requires a new way of thinking for most people. In over twenty years of teaching these methods, history shows that students who do not continue to use what they learned often revert back to old, ineffective habits. Changing our lifetime strategies of storytelling and categorization is very difficult without help. Over the years, we tried many ways to overcome this, but we had limited success at institutionalizing better problem solving. RealityCharting® software and RealityCharting Coach were created specifically to help solve this problem by first providing a simple user-friendly charting tool and a fun, fast learning guide in RealityCharting Coach.

Effective Solutions for Everyday Problems Every Time

Whether you are a professional incident investigator, a manager, or a line worker, RealityCharting® will help you understand your problem better than you have ever been able to understand it before. As a result of this understanding, you are able to find more effective solutions and to effectively communicate the value of those solutions to others. Because the RealityCharting process does not allow storytelling, the normal arguing and politics associated with problem solving are avoided. Clear evidence-based causal relationships are very hard to argue with and the RealityCharting process encourages diverse ideas and viewpoints such that the best solutions can be found together, as a team. The bottom line is this: Using RealityCharting® results in higher quality solutions in less time.

To get started using the RealityCharting® software you can download a trial version at http://www.realitycharting.com/downloads/demo.

About the Author

Dean L. Gano is president of Apollonian Publications, LLC, which is dedicated to helping others become the best event-based problem solvers they can be by providing highly effective problem-solving tools in the form of books and computer software. Mr. Gano brings more than forty years of experience in process industries, power plants, and computer software development to this endeavor. He started his incident investigation work and subsequent fascination with problem solving while working on solutions to the incident at Three-Mile Island Nuclear Power Station in the late 1970s.

Gano has participated in hundreds of incident investigations since then and has studied the human problem-solving process ever since. His unique version of effective problem solving has been taught to people from over 2,000 companies around the world for more than twenty years. The RealityCharting process is being taught in seven major languages on five continents and is being used globally by many of the Fortune 500 companies, the National Aeronautics and Space Administration, the Federal Aviation Administration, and other government entities.

Mr. Gano holds bachelor of science degrees in mechanical engineering and general science, was formerly certified as a nuclear reactor operator, and is a Vietnam veteran. He is a senior member of the American Society for Quality and the American Society of Safety Engineers. He is a philosopher and student who finds great happiness in learning and in helping others become more successful in their life pursuits.